Louisa County

VIRGINIA

Louisa County

VIRGINIA

A Brief History

Pattie Gordon Pavlansky Cooke

THE History PRESS

Published by The History Press
Charleston, SC 29403
www.historypress.net

First published 2008

Manufactured in the United States

ISBN 978.1.59629.376.2

Library of Congress CIP data applied for.

Notice: The information in this book is true and complete to the best of our knowledge. It is offered without guarantee on the part of the author or The History Press. The author and The History Press disclaim all liability in connection with the use of this book.

Dedicated to the Memory of Griswold Boxley.

Contents

Acknowledgements

The help of the following people and organizations was much appreciated: the Louisa Town Council, Mayor Jim Artz, Carter Cooke, Mary Minor, John Nolin, Marjorie Lee Woolfolk, Dickie Leake, Jimmy Talley, Mrs. Aubrey Seay, Gerald Harlow, Ann Avery Hunter, Nancy Woolfolk Agee, Frances Atkins, Brian Marks, Jessica Ellis, Breese Glennon, John Purcell, Susan Hopkins, the clerk of Louisa County Circuit Court, Christine Southard, Ashland Fortune, John Thomasson, Hattie Crebbs, John Gilmer and Steve Railann. Edited by Kate Cooke Sadler.

Note on Terminology

Going to Louisa.

In diaries, letters and notes, this phrase is used over and over by people living in Bumpass, Boswell's Tavern and Buckner. Even though those areas are part of Louisa County, the phrase was used to indicate that they were going to the courthouse. To understand Louisa County, one must know the village, the courthouse and the town of Louisa.

Chapter 1

The Indians and the Settlement of Louisa County

Louisa County is in the heart of Virginia. The county is beyond the fall line, which put Louisa beyond the easy reach of early settlers. The fall line is the point where the upland joins the lowland at a waterfall, and where ships ended their inland progress. Cities such as Fredericksburg and Richmond, located at the fall line, grew naturally. Louisa County is located in the Piedmont and the town of Louisa proper is a little west of the center of the county. The rolling hills of the Piedmont separate the tidewater from the Blue Ridge Mountains. The waterways of the tidewater were the easiest means of travel, but the Piedmont lacked this advantage. When travel was harder, cities grew slowly. Therefore, Louisa County was not the most advantageous area for settlement. The town grew up entirely as an adjunct to the courthouse.

Native Americans created the first man-made boundaries in Louisa. In his *Notes on the State of Virginia*, Thomas Jefferson reveals that the Monacan Indians lived between the James River and the headwaters of the Pamunkey. The Monacans were a confederacy of five tribes. The tribe living in Louisa County, Fluvanna County and near Charlottesville was called Monasiccapanoe (or Monasukapanough). The Monacan language has been traced to a Siouan strain, which means the Monacans were related to the Indians of the West and are believed to be from the Ohio Valley.

According to oral tradition, a Native American village was located at the Louisa Town spring at Donnally Dale. There has been no authority or archaeological study to substantiate this claim. Evidently, a field located in Donnally Dale between what are now Simms Avenue and Patrick Henry Drive was a treasure-trove of Indian arrowheads for the local schoolchildren of the 1930s. People can still find arrowheads there today. There were trappers and frontier families living in Louisa before 1700. By 1720, land in Louisa had been patented or deeded, which proved that the county was being settled. The settlers came up from Hanover County or up the North Anna from Spotsylvania County. As Tidewater settlers moved westward, they formed counties for political, administrative and judicial purposes. The settlers needed to build roads, to grant licenses for inns and mills and to record deeds to land. As each new county was formed, it was given no western border. When settlers went so far beyond the courthouse of the previous county that they could not reach the courthouse easily,

Four arrowheads found within a block of Donnally's field less than twenty years ago.

a new county was formed. So in 1700, the area that is called Louisa County today was a part of New Kent County. In 1721, Hanover County was carved out of New Kent County, so Louisa then became a part of Hanover County. And in 1742, Louisa became a county in its own right when it was divided from Hanover. Roads were created out of the wilderness that was Louisa from original Indian and game paths. The Virginia House of Burgesses passed an act to form Louisa County. To begin the process, the inhabitants presented a petition in Williamsburg to the Virginia House of Burgesses on December 11, 1738, to prepare a bill to make Upper Hanover into a separate county (Louisa). After its introduction and three readings, this bill became an act on June 9, 1740. The act was passed "due to many inconveniences which attend the upper inhabitants of the county of Hanover, by reason of their great distance from the Courthouse."[1] And so a new county was created.

In May of 1742, Louisa County was named in honor of Princess Louise, the youngest child of George II and Queen Caroline of England; the small settlement was named Louisa Courthouse. Louise was their fifth and youngest daughter. Born on December 18 or 19 of 1724, she grew up to be a happy and lively young woman. On December 11, 1743, Princess Louise married the Crown Prince Frederick of

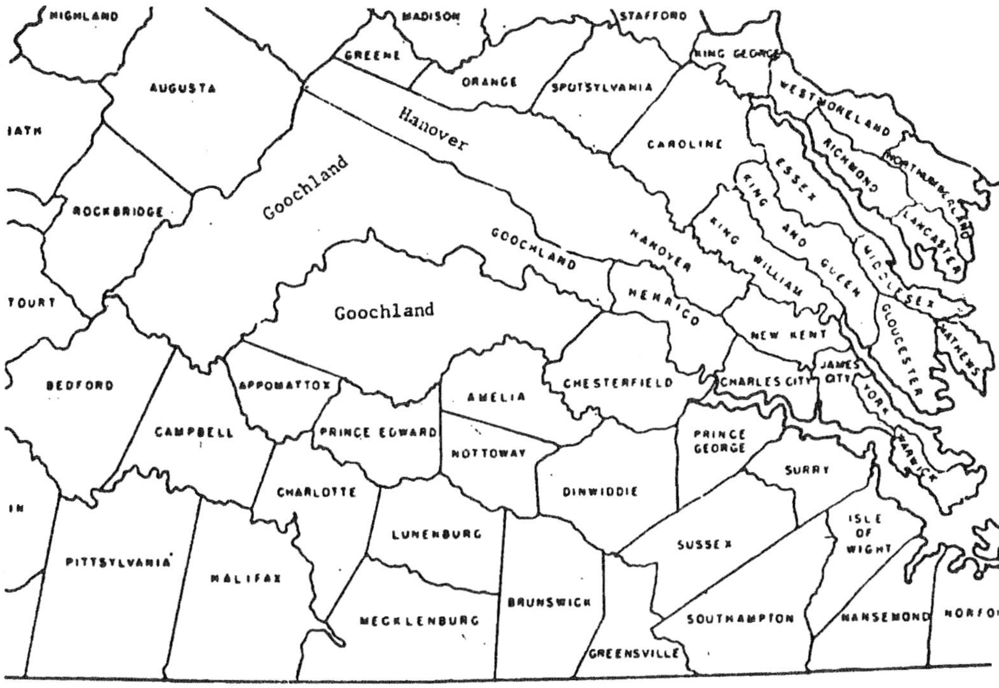

Hanover and Goochland Counties, circa 1740. They comprised the future Louisa and Albemarle Counties.

Denmark. By 1746, she was Queen Louise of Denmark and Norway. In less than ten years after her marriage, Queen Louise died in childbirth on December 19, 1751. She had given birth to several children, some of whose descendants live in the United States today.[2]

In November 1742, Louisa County was directed by the Virginia House of Burgesses Executive Council to hold court at the house of Matthew Jouett. The original records of 1742 can be found today in the present Louisa County Courthouse. Matthew Jouett's courthouse was not in the same location as the present courthouse.

The first page of the December 13, 1742 Louisa County Order Book reads: "At the House of Matthew Jouett, Gent., on Beaver Creek in the County of Louisa the XIII day of December in the XVI day of year of the Reign of our Sovereign Lord George the second, by the Grace of God of Great Britain, France, Ireland, King, Defender of the Faith, etc. Anno Dom. MDCCXLII."

Also appointed to the county court was the clerk, who recorded all the business of the court. Colonel James Littlepage of Hanover County was the first clerk of Louisa County. He traveled back and forth from Hanover to Louisa to conduct county business.

In 1743, the first courthouse was built on the land of Matthew Jouett on Beaver Creek at his expense. In these early years of the county, the government was not concentrated at one location as it is today. Matthew Jouett lived on Beaver Creek and the sheriff and jail were situated closer to Buckner. It is possible that the courthouse remained at Beaver

Creek until the courthouse tract was owned by James Littlepage, the county clerk. It was certainly moved no later than 1757, when purchased by Thomas Johnson.

Monthly county courts were important occasions in the business and social life of the county. The meetings prompted gatherings of large numbers of people, which led to sales and private business transactions, and they provided relief from the loneliness of rural farm life.

At the first meeting of the Louisa Court, Joseph Bickley Jr. was appointed sheriff of Louisa County and ordered to "undertake the building of a Jail" on his property. The location of Joseph Bickley's home was in the vicinity of Swifts Mill on Little River.[3] The jail was built by March 14, 1743, and used for three years. At that time, it was realized that the cost and time for transporting prisoners between the courthouse and jail were too high. A new jail was built in 1745 at the site of the courthouse on the land of Matthew Jouett. These first jails were supplied with stocks and pillories, a whipping post and a ducking stool.

After appointments were made, the business of running the county began. Matthew Jouett was granted a license to keep an ordinary. Ordinaries were rest stops for people traveling through the county—what we might call an inn today. The ordinaries of the 1700s were small, crowded affairs. It was not unusual for six men to sleep together in one bed—first come, first served. Matthew Jouett's ordinary was important for the people transacting business on court day.

Matthew Jouett died sometime between 1744 and June of 1746. The courthouse tract was bought by Robert Jennings of Hanover County and the Honorable Philip Lightfoot of York County from Jouett's executor, John Moore, in 1746.[4] At some point, James Littlepage became partial owner of the property. There may have been more courthouses after this but there is no record that locates or describes them individually. For the town of Louisa, a record of the location starts with the sale of the courthouse tract to Thomas Johnson. The history of the town revolves around the history of the courthouse and the nearby tavern. Much of the history is associated with the clerks of court who were in positions to amass large properties. Thomas Johnson's courthouse and tavern were located in proximity to the present courthouse and Cooke Building of today. This tract of land, upon which the town sits today, was bought after the death of Matthew Jouett by his executor. The tract contained 150 acres, owned by James Watson.[5] This tract was added to the Jouett Courthouse tract, "[p]aid in hand by Matthew Jouett, deceased [*sic*]," and was bought by Thomas Johnson of Caroline County and his wife Mary in July of 1752.[6]

Chapter 2

The Johnson Family and the Village of Louisa

Major Thomas Johnson was important in the history of the town and the county. The son of Thomas Johnson and Ann Meriwether, he moved to Louisa from Caroline County. According to genealogical records, he married Elizabeth Ashton in the 1740s (his wife is called Mary in the previously cited Jouett deed). Elizabeth and Thomas Johnson had several sons: Captain Thomas Johnson, Richard Johnson, Henry Ashton Johnson and George Johnson. By 1771, Thomas Johnson and his concubine Ursula Estes, widow of John Estes, had started another family. His ownership of the property lasted through the king's rule, the Revolution and the first stirrings of our new American country.

Thomas Johnson was Louisa's representative in the Virginia House of Burgesses from 1758 to 1771 and he served as a burgess with Patrick Henry in 1765. A "Thomas Johnson" represented Louisa intermittently after the Revolution, until 1783, when the House of Burgesses was renamed the Virginia General Assembly. Thomas Johnson was also named the sheriff of Louisa County and served as a burgess then, as well. A Thomas Johnson, courthouse property owner, achieved the rank of major during the Revolution. He was on the Committee of Safety and was a member of the ruling ranks of the county as a justice of the peace, becoming the chief justice and a vestryman by 1787. He and his son, Thomas Johnson Jr., were both county justices in the commonwealth in 1776.

By 1757, a new courthouse was built near the site of the present courthouse. If this is the same courthouse that survived until 1866, it is described by several depositions in the chancery case of *Arnette v. Cammack* in 1891.[7] The "Old Courthouse" is described by Hugh Cullen in an 1891 deposition as he knew it in 1844. The courthouse had a thirty-foot-long front and ran thirty feet to the rear. It was made up of three rooms and a front platform. A big chimney was situated between two of the rooms. This was undoubtedly a frame building positioned in the approximate location of the present Ogg building on the courthouse square, only perpendicular to it.

Thomas Johnson and his family were members of the Anglican religion, the only recognized religion under British rule in the colony of Virginia. A Louisa County historian, Ransome True, stated,

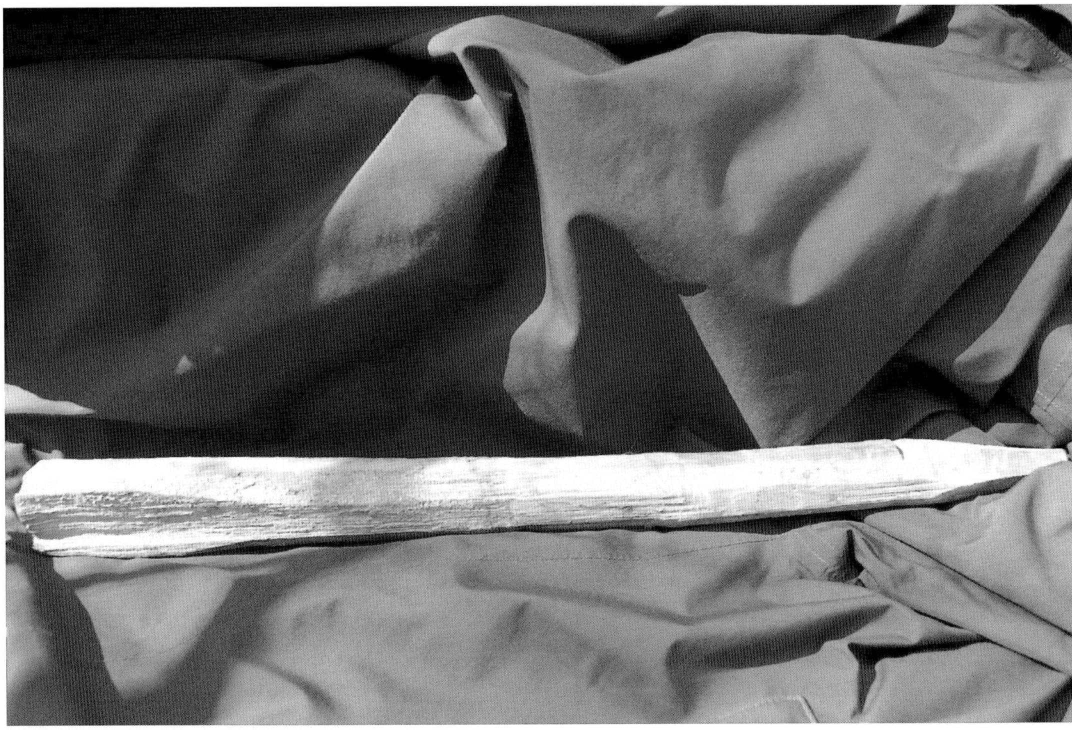

This tree nail at the Louisa Feed Store could be from the second courthouse. Sections of the second courthouse were used in the building of Bonavita's Store on the courthouse green; Bonavita's Store was dismantled by E.S. Hansen and moved to become the Louisa Feed Store in 1917.

Religion in Louisa was fundamentally different from religion in many other Virginia counties. There was an Anglican church in the county before the Revolution of which some important county families were members. But it was a weak church and quickly died once the church was disestablished and the glebe sold. The real strength of religion lay in the hands of dissenters.

Baptists, Presbyterians, Methodists and Quakers were at the time considered dissenters.

The buying of land and the operation of businesses were controlled by the king of England before the Revolution. The king also required that the land be divided into parishes. In England, a parish was a community or neighborhood. In Virginia, a parish was a division of land over which an Anglican minister was the authority figure. Parishes were often formed before or at the same time as counties, with similar boundaries. There was no freedom of religion in Virginia and the Church of England, the Anglican Church, was established by law in Virginia. Each parish was ruled by a vestry of twelve men, presided over by the minister. Taxes were imposed by the vestry in order to pay the minister's salary and to build churches. The vestry was also responsible for the relief of the poor. All settlers were required to attend church at least once a month or they were fined. Louisa was in St. Martins Parish until 1742, when it became Fredericksville Parish and a county.

Hardship made religion a particularly important part of colonial life. Louisa played a large part in a religious revolution that had started in Hanover County in the 1740s. This movement was called the "Great Awakening" and it was a serious threat by dissenters to the system of authority that had been formed in Virginia. Part of the conflict was directed against the gentry, who were justices of peace and vestry members. Quakers were the first religious group of note to settle Louisa County, as early as 1746. The Presbyterians established Providence Church in the 1740s. "The real fire in Louisa religion was still to come. In the 1760s several Louisa citizens became converted by Baptist revivalists preaching in Culpeper and other nearby places."[8] These evangelicals rejected the horse racing, gambling, cockfighting and dancing of the gentry class. The new religions espoused the communal experience of self-criticism and questioned personal behavior. Louisa County was a haven for these dissenting religions. In many counties, and at times in Louisa, revolutionary ministers were beaten and jailed.

It was in this atmosphere that the Reverend James Maury brought religious matters to a head when he opposed a member of the Johnson family. James Maury was born in 1718. In 1751, he became minister to Fredericksville Parish and continued to serve until his death on June 9, 1769. On August 9, 1755, Mr. Maury, father to ten children, wrote that he was in financial straits and that money was scarce. The Reverend Maury stated, "I am planted about two miles to the northeast of Walker's in Louisa." Today this area is in Albemarle County, but until 1762 it was in Louisa. Maury kept a private school in Louisa where he taught five boys who later became signers of the Declaration of Independence.[9] Thomas Jefferson was one of his students and, ironically, later established freedom of religion in Virginia.

In October 1758, the Virginia General Assembly passed legislation concerning the price of tobacco and the rate of payment to the clergy that became known as the Two-Penny Act.[10] The clergy had been paid in tobacco rather than money, which meant the clergy could sell at the best rate. By creating a fixed rate of two pence per pound, their salaries were reduced. When the colonial government refused to rescind this law, the clergy went to King George, who refused to recognize the law.

Sheriff Thomas Johnson, the tax collector and nephew of Thomas Johnson (owner of the courthouse tract), refused to pay the Reverend Maury. Maury then went to the vestry and they too refused his demands in 1761. It might be noted that the vestry were essentially the same as the justices of the peace. Vestry meetings were held at Louisa Courthouse so it is certain that there were clashes there between the main characters in this drama. When the Reverend Maury brought his suit to Hanover Courthouse in April 1762, he won the original case. In the second suit, where damages were assessed, he was awarded minimal recompense, which essentially meant a loss for him.

Sheriff Thomas Johnson brought Patrick Henry to Louisa County and the town. He hired him as an attorney to argue the compensation to be given to the Reverend Maury. In a speech during the trial at Hanover Courthouse, Patrick Henry attacked the tyranny of King George and the church and state. Cries of treason were heard from the audience but he convinced the jury, and they awarded only one penny to the Reverend Maury. This case brought Patrick Henry to prominence and began his association with Louisa County and the town of Louisa.

From the *Central Virginian*, March 5, 1981: "A group of children from the old Louisa High School celebrated Patrick Henry's birthday by a celebration at Henry's Louisa homeplace, 'Roundabout.'" The picture was probably taken around 1910. Roundabout began to decay after that time. *Courtesy of the* Central Virginian.

In 1762, the county lines of Louisa were reformed so that the western portion of Louisa stretched to Albemarle County, the same boundaries the county has today. For this reason, the Louisa Courthouse was no longer in the exact center of the county. The parish lines also changed by an act of the Virginia General Assembly, causing Louisa to be in Trinity Parish and Albemarle to be in Fredericksville Parish.[11]

It was after this that Louisa County elected Patrick Henry as its representative in the House of Burgesses. It was during his brief residence in Louisa County (1765–1768) at Roundabout that he made his immortal speech in the House of Burgesses against the Stamp Act. In the climax of this speech, he cried, "Caesar had his Brutus, Charles the First his Cromwell, and George III—may profit by their example. If that be treason, make the most of it!"[12]

Patrick Henry took an oath as an Anglican vestryman in 1766 in Louisa.[13] George Morgan, in his biography of Patrick Henry, stated that Henry "always walked to court, carrying his gun, and hunting by the way.[14]...After the hunt, he would go to Louisa Court clad in a coarse cloth coat, greasy leather breeches, and a pair of saddle bags on his arms."[15] Patrick Henry walked down some of the same streets in the town of Louisa that we walk today. The roadways of the time were essentially in the same location as roads today.

In 1764, a complaint was made by Major Thomas Johnson that John Carr and Samuel Ragland desired to have the courthouse removed to another, more central location. The courthouse is described as "an ordinary house and many stables and convenient house of entertainment fit for the reception of guests by which the plaintiff (Johnson) did make a considerable gain and profit by Keeping."[16] The ordinary or tavern is believed to have been located very close to the Louisa Hotel, presently the Cooke Building.

County courts were held on the second Monday of the month, quarterly—in March, June, August and November. On these occasions, a portable town would grow at the courthouse, with carts and carriages carrying people and goods there. March was a particularly important time as it came at the end of winter. With inadequate roads, most people spent much of the winter on their isolated farms.

Chapter 3

The Courthouse and the Revolution

Dabney Carr, born in Louisa County at Bear Castle, represented Louisa in the House of Burgesses in the place of Thomas Johnson from 1772 to 1773.[17] Carr's chief contribution was the introduction of the Carr Resolution to set up a Committee of Correspondence between the colonies. His resolution was approved by the Burgesses, and the Virginia Committee wrote to the other twelve colonies urging them to keep in touch with each other. A letter to parliament, drafted by Carr, stated: "No subject of Great Britain can justly be made obedient to laws without their personal consent or by the consent of their representative." This was a great step forward in colonial cooperation.

Living in Louisa County, which was so isolated by the difficulty in transportation, must have influenced Dabney Carr's idea of intercommunication. The county residents were dependent on court days and church days for their information on the coming revolution. Dabney Carr also passed a resolution for the formation of Committees of Safety in 1773 in each county. Louisa appointed a committee in May of 1775.[18] The members were loyal to the cause of freedom. The Louisa members included Thomas Walker, James Dabney, Samuel Ragland, Waddy Thompson, Thomas Johnson Jr., Nathaniel Anderson, Richard Anderson, William White, Charles Barret, William Pettus, Lancelot Minor, Thomas Johnson Sr., John Crutchfield and Charles Smith. In this and a later committee the Johnson family was prominent.

Thomas Johnson was a delegate to the Virginia Convention in 1775. He was present for Patrick Henry's "Give me liberty or give me death" speech at St. John's Church in Richmond and he supported Patrick Henry consistently.

The Louisa County Committee of Safety met and sent a letter to the *Virginia Gazette*, which was published in Williamsburg in 1775. The letter was written in response to Governor Dunmore emptying the gunpowder from the colony's magazine and in support of Patrick Henry. Governor Dunmore, as the king's representative in Virginia, was in direct opposition to Patrick Henry and the colonists.

> *This committee being fully sensible of the benefits that may redound to the community in general from the spirited behaviour* [sic] *of Captain Patrick Henry, and the other officers and Gentlemen*

Jack Jouett silhouette.

> *soldiers of the volunteer company of Hanover, in procuring satisfaction for the gunpowder taken out of the colony's magazine, beg leave to return them our most hearty thanks.*

Thomas Johnson's four sons answered the call for support during the Revolution. Thomas Johnson Jr. was in the Third Regiment and appointed captain on September 9, 1776. His brother Henry Ashton became second lieutenant on April 10, 1779, under James Watson. George was sworn in as lieutenant in the militia on June 12, 1780, and Richard achieved second lieutenant on March 17, 1781.[19] "Louisa was invaded by both the British and the American forces, the former under Cornwallis and the latter under Lafayette, in May and June of 1781."[20]

Jack Jouett was born in Albemarle County in 1754 after his grandfather, Matthew Jouett, moved out of Louisa County, but Jack certainly knew the courthouse well. His father was deputy, or sub-sheriff, of Louisa County from 1762 to 1763.[21] His father also had a plantation near Cuckoo.[22] His rough ride from Cuckoo, Louisa County, has been called the single greatest act of heroism of the war. In June of 1781, Jack Jouett learned that British General Tarleton was on his way to Charlottesville to capture Thomas Jefferson and the Virginia General Assembly. Richmond had fallen to the British, and Governor Jefferson, Patrick Henry and other notable legislators had gone to Charlottesville and Monticello with plans to reconvene the General Assembly in Charlottesville. Jack Jouett knew that Banastre Tarleton would take the road through the courthouse, so he cut over to Three Chopt Road.

Tarleton stopped just beyond the Louisa Courthouse to burn a dozen wagons holding supplies for the Continentals and he rested there for three hours. Jack Jouett was able to beat him to Charlottesville and warn Thomas Jefferson and the others. Jack Jouett's mission was successful, and Jefferson and the lawmakers escaped to meet later in Staunton, Virginia. While Jack Jouett was racing to warn Jefferson, the denizens of the courthouse were witnesses to Tarleton's ride through what would one day become the town of Louisa.

The second incursion into Louisa by troops was led by a Frenchman, the Marquis de Lafayette. Lafayette traveled through Louisa in June of 1781 and stopped at Boswell's Tavern. Lafayette was made a major general by the Continental Congress. He was in Louisa to keep his troops between the British forces and the supplies to the west. The road he traveled to check the British movement was for some time called the Marquis Road. The presence of Lafayette caused General Cornwallis of the British army to end his westward movement and turn back toward Richmond.

Major Thomas Johnson's tavern was offered to the troops who had come from the surrounding area to help the Marquis de Lafayette. Mr. Johnson also fed the Albemarle and Spotsylvania militia and furnished fodder and pasture for cattle and horses.[23]

In the same year, on October 19, Lord Cornwallis was defeated at Yorktown and sent his sword to George Washington. The Revolution had been virtually won, but despite the peace treaty with Britain, the war did not officially end until 1783. King George III refused to acknowledge defeat for some time.

Chapter 4
Location, Location, Location
Thomas Johnson and the Tavern

Thomas Johnson was a character of the first water. He immediately built a tavern near the courthouse to accommodate the visitors on court days. The court met every month, with special sessions held four times a year. It took some county residents a full day's trip to reach the courthouse and they needed a place to stay. Other services certainly must have been available around the courthouse as well. The need for stables was a certainty.

Baron Ludwig von Closen, traveling with General Rochambeau, mentioned Johnson's tavern in February of 1782 in his journal.

> *In the evening we slept at Louisa Courthouse, in the house of a certain Thomas Johnson, a former Major in the militia. I can truthfully say that I have never seen a dirtier, more shocking, and more stinking barracks than that of this major, who himself, was the greatest pig that earth ever produced. Not one of us could shut an eye throughout the night. The general* [Rochambeau], *who alone could have a bed, was eaten by vermin, and we who slept on straw had our ears tickled by rats!*[24]

Though Thomas Johnson's amenities may not have been appreciated, he was a very powerful person, as was his family.

A couple of months later, General Chastellux visited Thomas Johnson's ordinary, despite a warning from General Rochambeau, because he was curious.

> *Under the pretence of inquiring for the road, I went in, and saw that there was no other lodging for travelers than the landlord's own room. This man, called Mr. Johnson, has become so monstrously fat that he can no longer move out of his armchair. He is a good humored fellow, whose manners are not very strict, who has loved good cheer and all sorts of pleasures to such an extent that at the age of fifty he has so augmented his bulk and diminished his fortune, that by two opposite principles he is near seeing the termination of both; but all this does not in the least affect his gaiety. I found him stretched out in his armchair, which serves him for a bed; for it would be difficult for him to lie down, and impossible to rise. A stool supported his enormous legs, in which were large fissures on each side, a prelude to what must soon happen*

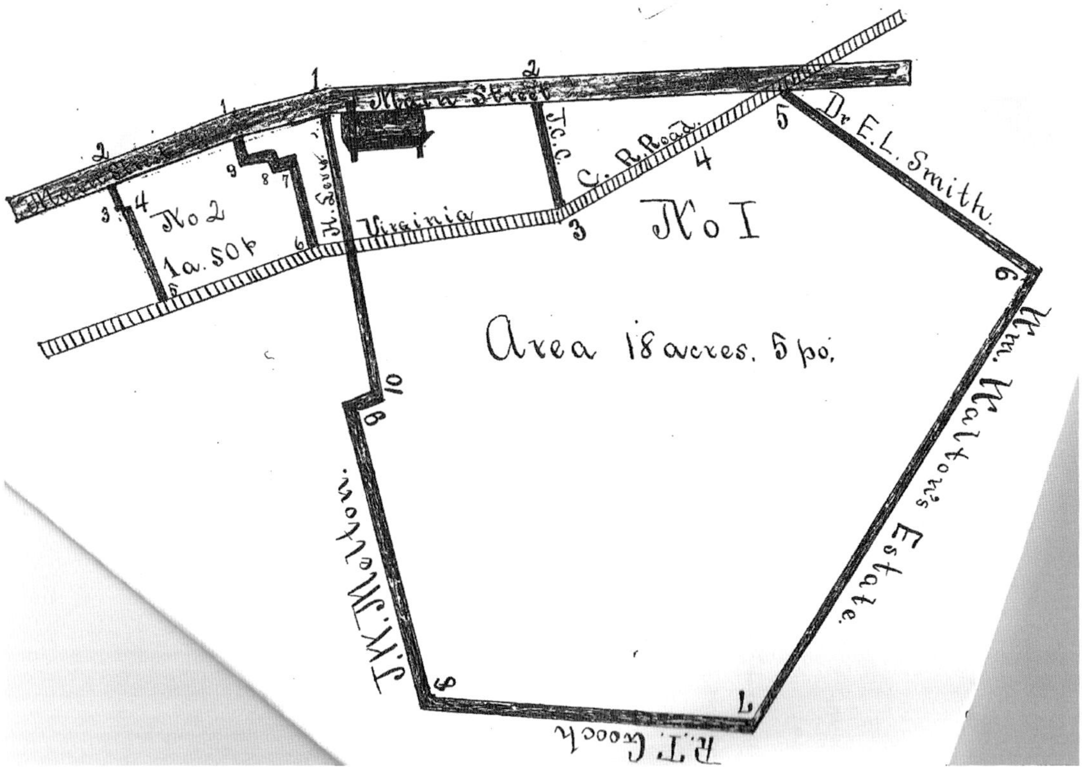

In 1862, the tavern lot included much of the northern side of Main Street and only excluded Hyman Levy's lot. That the tavern lot was still intact after over one hundred years indicates its importance to the town. *Courtesy of the Louisa County Circuit Court Clerk's Office.*

> *to his belly. A large ham and a "bowl of grog" served him for company, like a man resolved to die surrounded by his friends.*[25]

Major Johnson surpassed all expectations and lived until 1798, leaving behind land and money.[26]

The censuses of 1782 and 1785 give a good sense of the courthouse area. In 1782, there were "14 white souls and 16 black souls" listed under Thomas Johnson. In 1785, there were "15 white souls" and, more importantly, "five dwelling houses and seventeen out buildings."[27] The Louisa Land Tax Book listed Thomas Johnson with 2,410 acres in 1782.

In 1787, Thomas Johnson once again had to fight off a campaign to move the courthouse to a more central location. Some 339 people signed a petition to have the courthouse moved. Thomas Johnson's reply to this petition is interesting because he implies that the petition was brought forward partly on religious grounds:

> *Which petition being signed by divers persons calling themselves Baptists was procured by your petitioner, who used every act and specie of low cunning to entice even Boys and Men to sign same and many of whom have since retracted protesting their sorrow at signing a petition*

> *to deprive any citizen of his property*[...]*That in 1764 a petition of the same tendency was drawn for lucrative motives, whereupon the council gave instructions that the county be measured*[...]*Whereupon the council approved this site for its abundance of water and salubrity of its situation and the commodiousness thereof. Signed Thomas Johnson.*[28]

Historian Ransome True describes the controversy, "Although they had a good grounds for their desires, namely that the courthouse had been used as a storehouse, and the jail as a stable by Thomas Johnson on whose land they stood, they lost. Whether there was an equal number who opposed is not known. However, they had the clinching argument in the fact that the same Thomas Johnson was the Chief Justice and he was too fat to get on a horse. Consequently, although he could waddle over to the courthouse from his ordinary, he would have been unable to continue as chief justice if the courthouse were moved."[29] Johnson won and the courthouse has stayed in the same spot up to the present day.

In December 1788, Sheriff James Meriwether presented an objection to receiving prisoners—there was no jail.[30] A new brick jail was to be erected on the land of Thomas Johnson. Thomas Johnson felt the county plans were his concern, "Thomas Johnson, gent, objects the letting a prison other than a stone prison agreeable to the order of the last Court—also he objects to their letting one for a Gaoler to live in, to introduce family on his land, as he thinks it illegal."[31] Sheriff Meriwether continued to complain of the inadequacy of the jail. Another jail was built at some point since by August of 1789, repairs were already necessary.

In 1792, it was reiterated that a duty of the court was to build and maintain a courthouse, jail, pillory, whipping post, stocks and a ducking stool if necessary. The jail's function was mainly to house debtors up until 1850. Criminals were punished at the pillory and whipping post. Murderers were hanged.

On April 3, 1789, "a plat of the prison bounds was this day received, likewise two acres of land laid off agreeable to an Act of Assembly for the use of this County." This was recorded in the Louisa County Order Book. The public land was not officially sold to the county until 1818.

Again in 1805, a building contract was chosen for a new jail. This new brick building was completed to the satisfaction of the building inspectors by November of 1807. The new jail was located across the present-day Main Street and a few yards west of the present courthouse. It cost $500, plus an additional $450 to redo the second story. Public and private construction reflected the new values of a county coming of age as part of the new United States of America.

Chapter 5

John Poindexter and Adjustments as Americans

John Poindexter was the personification of the religious environment in Louisa County after the Revolution. He was strong-willed, antislavery and wealthy, and as county clerk and member of an old Louisa family, he was politically powerful. He spelled the end of the Episcopal Church's domination in Louisa. He became county clerk in 1790, one year after George Washington was elected president of the United States.

Many Quakers had moved out of Louisa County by 1790, but there were still some families left. The Presbyterians remained, but after the Revolution, the Baptists attracted the largest number of new members. Methodist circuit riders were just beginning their conversions.

John Poindexter Jr. was appointed clerk of Louisa County Court on January 11, 1790. He was the first clerk of the Louisa Court who was born and raised in Louisa—it is fitting that his influence should have been so great. John Poindexter was also the clerk of the Circuit Court of Law from the formation of that court in 1819. The establishment of circuit courts weakened the strength of the county courts. Although there were several changes in the county court system made while John Poindexter was in office, he retained the power to prepare the court dockets.

John Poindexter was also very influential as a Baptist minister. Thomas Jefferson was a leader in passing "an Act for Establishing Religious Freedom in 1786," which required that the Anglican Church be disestablished and its lands sold after the Revolution. When John Poindexter became clerk in 1790, he professed the Anglican religion and barely tolerated the Baptists. Through the influence of his wife, Elizabeth Thornton Johnson, daughter of Sheriff Johnson, he was converted to the Baptist religion by August of 1790 and baptized. By February 1792, he was ordained to the work of the Baptist ministry. His "conversion was met by extreme cynicism in the county until his hospitality reached such proportions that the tide turned in his favor."[32] John Poindexter's conversion and ministry led many to follow him into the Baptist religion.

John Poindexter is also worthy of note for the emancipation of his slaves. He once stated:

This building, close to Roundabout Castle, home of Sheriff Thomas Johnson in the Quail area, is believed to be an early county clerk's office. John Poindexter, the third county clerk, used it when the law required the office to be kept not more than five measured miles from the courthouse.

> *I, John Poindexter, of Louisa County and State of Virginia being convinced of the injustice and impropriety of Slavery and also convinced that the practice of slave holding is in direct opposition to and violation of that holy precept delivered from the lips of the Lord Jesus Christ himself (in whom I trust my all). Therefore as ye would that men should do unto you so do ye also unto them, for this is the law and the prophets.*[33]

Following his words with actions, Reverend John Poindexter began to free his enslaved people from the sixth day of October 1794 to the end of his life. To ensure that release occurred after his death, John Poindexter recorded manumission papers in county or district courts and a copy was sent to the "present humane society" of the state or any society of that kind. The Benevolent Society, of which he was a member, was created to secure humane treatment and eventual manumission of slaves. Reverend Poindexter did not free the enslaved people he held until they had completed a required length of service on his plantation. Most of the enslaved people completed this service by the age of twenty-one.

Following the example of John Poindexter, on April 4, 1806, Ralph Quarles presented to the court a deed of manumission to liberate his slaves Lucy and Maria.[34] Lucy was the mother of John Mercer Langston and this act by his father, Ralph Quarles, allowed Langston to become one of Virginia's most distinguished black leaders. Since Mr. Langston was born circa 1829, he was born free and left Louisa in 1834.

Before the new American postal service went into effect, public letters going inland were carried from plantation to plantation to the hands of the right person, carried by responsible people traveling in the same direction. Benjamin Franklin was the first postmaster general of the postal service, created in 1775. "Post" roads were established in Louisa County prior to 1799. On December 2, 1799, in "an Act to alter and establish sundry post roads," a road was named running "from Fredericksburg, by Spotsylvania Court House, and Louisa Court House, to Columbia." This post road connected the James and Rappahannock Rivers and evidently served places along the route. Today this road is Route 208, running from Fredericksburg to Ware's Cross Roads or Dickinson's Store, and from Louisa to Columbia. The post road recognized Louisa Courthouse as an established settlement and indicates that the main road to Louisa at this time was not the Richmond road but the Fredericksburg road. Ludlum Branham was the first postmaster of Louisa Courthouse and served for one year. He was followed by William Lawrence from 1801 to 1803 and Henry Lawrence from 1803 to 1818.

The Revolution did not change the qualifications of voters, and the franchise still rested upon property ownership. Male citizens over twenty-one years of age could vote if they owned twenty-five acres of land with a twelve-foot-square house, fifty acres of wild land or a town lot. Those who lived in rented property in the village of Louisa did not have the franchise unless they owned land elsewhere. As time progressed, the courts that were made up of the wealthiest families before the Revolution welcomed small planters to their ranks and later, tavern keepers, merchants and lawyers.[35]

"As the population of the county increased, so did the business of the court."[36] As the business of the county took longer to complete, more people came to the courthouse for longer periods. "In turn, their presence brought many more people and the courthouse, courthouse green, ordinary and adjacent areas became the premier business center for the county."[37]

Chapter 6

Henry Lawrence and a Village Begins

On January 28, 1807, the Johnson family sold to Henry Lawrence the courthouse tract of 397 acres, upon which stood both the old and the new courthouse.[38] One of the boundaries was William Crawford's blacksmith shop that today would not be part of the village but would nevertheless be located within town boundaries. Henry Lawrence was probably already living at the courthouse since he was the postmaster from 1803 to 1818.

Henry Lawrence made the first commercial division of the courthouse tract in an 1816 sale to Benjamin Willis of a two-acre lot of land. Benjamin Willis was born in Louisa County in 1776. He was the son of Reuben Willis and Ann Garnett of Orange County. The land is described as that "on which the said Willis now resides in the occupancy of a merchant, near the tavern."[39] This proves to us that others were, in fact, living and working at the courthouse tract before this time, perhaps in rented stores and houses. The land is further described as adjoining the public square, which means that there was one store on the land kept by someone other than Henry Lawrence.

In 1816, a second deed was initiated by Lawrence that stated the restrictions on the use of land at Louisa Courthouse. It was agreed between the parties that the "said Willis, nor any other person for him, should suffer to be sold, any thing that might in any way interfere or injure the said Lawrence's tavern kept at the said Court house. The said Willis should not keep on the said 'lott' of ground, a tavern boarding house, stabliage, nor in any manner retail spirits of any kind, wines of any sort, beer, porter, cider, or any sort of drinks made thereof. And that he should not keep a house of entertainment."[40] If Benjamin Willis did any of the above, the deed would be void. The restrictions applied to all property sold at the courthouse until 1904.

Why Henry Lawrence felt it necessary to implement these restrictions is unknown. It is known that Waddy Lipscomb had a tavern before 1824, located somewhere between West Street and Sims Avenue. James Beadles owned a building called "the hotel," listed in the 1805 assurance policy, which was located on Fredericksburg Avenue.[41] Job Harris bought seventy-five acres on Beaver Creek from James Beadles and applied for a tavern license from 1802 until 1807, which his wife Jane continued until 1814 and their son after that. Was the area inundated with taverns? It would be a good reason for the restrictions within the village itself. Generally taverns, country stores and so forth would not be established less than five miles (the equivalent of one day's journey) from one another. All that competition within a mile would be daunting to merchants. Henry Lawrence may have desired to distinguish between public land and his private land. In 1816, Henry Lawrence and John Poindexter were appointed as additional commissioners to contract for "the building and erecting of said Courthouse and Offices at Louisa Courthouse."[42] As owner of the courthouse property, Henry Lawrence was involved in county matters.

In December, Lawrence made the second sale to a merchant. He sold one acre to "an alien friend," Alexander Levy, for $1,000.[43] The lot was described as located "nearly opposite the courthouse near the horse rack, and public road."[44] The property line ran through Lawrence's icehouse.

John Poindexter vouched for Alexander Levy since he was not an American. Since Levy was not a citizen, he could not legally receive or hold title to land. Levy was a Frenchman of the Jewish religion said to have emigrated from France to avoid persecution there. He declared his intention to become a citizen in 1817 and did so in 1826. It was stated that he had good moral character, "attached to the principles of the constitution," and that he renounced allegiance to any foreign state.[45] He had a store in the village but lived a couple of miles from the courthouse. His home was later sold to the county to become the poorhouse.

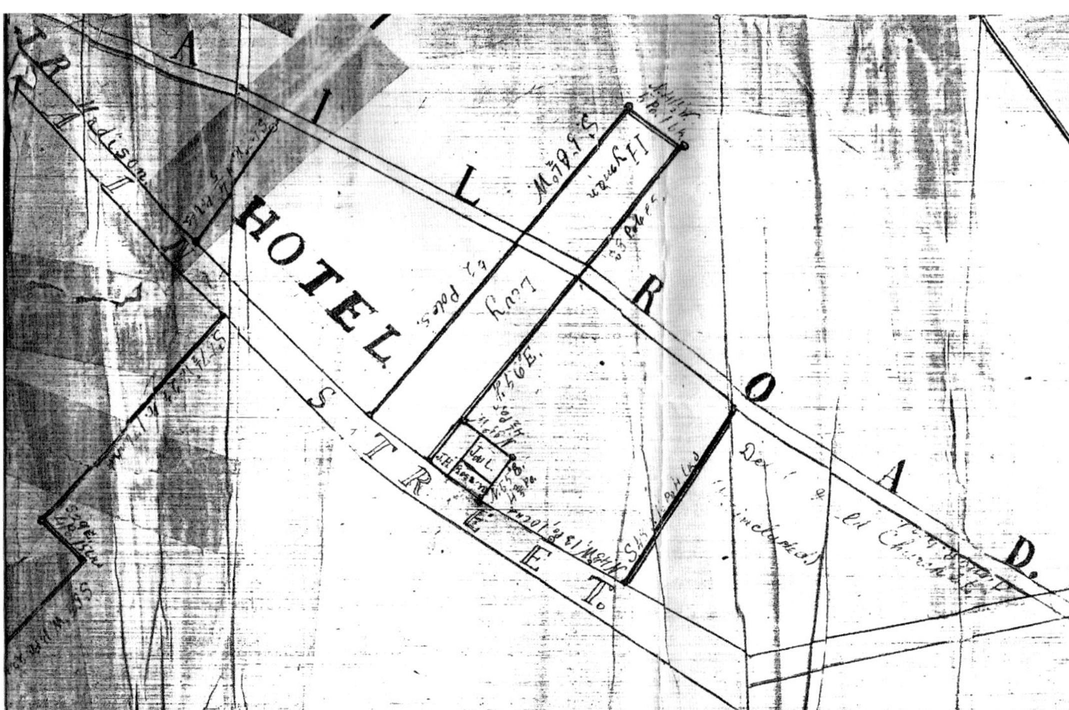

A map of Elisha Melton's property in 1854 shows the position of Hyman Levy's land, which was owned by the Levy family for almost a hundred years with the same property lines. Included are the jail and the business of John Rosson. *Courtesy of the Louisa County Circuit Court Clerk's Office.*

In 1818, the third courthouse building was built. It was located just in front of the site of the present courthouse. It was built of brick and remained the Louisa Courthouse until 1905, when the present courthouse was built. A new courthouse was very important to the county in 1818 because this was where people met to transact business, hold court cases and record deeds. The courthouse was almost as important as a meeting and business center as it was for the legal and political functions that occurred there. There was enough county business that a separate building for county records became necessary. This building was later erected as a place for the clerk to record and maintain the county deeds and wills. No picture of the clerk's office exists.

Henry Lawrence was appointed by the county to "keep the courthouse of Louisa County," like Matthew Jouett and Thomas Johnson before him.[46] Lawrence was also jailor for the county. And so the personal, county and village affairs continued to be intertwined.

On October 12, 1818, Henry Lawrence officially sold to the Louisa County Gentlemen Justices the "lot of land upon which the courthouse now stands," comprising two acres.[47] He also conveyed land upon which the new jail stood, and ten feet all around the said jail. Though plats (maps) of the public square had been drawn in June of 1816 and earlier, for the first time the county officially owned the land upon which the courthouse stood.

Henry Lawrence was responsible for the restrictions on the courthouse land, for the first sale of two parcels of land containing three acres near the courthouse and for the

Louisa Courthouse, built in 1818, as depicted by Elmer S. Burruss. This picture can be found in the Louisa County Courthouse. *Courtesy of the Louisa County Circuit Court Clerk's Office.*

sale of the public square to the county. It was under his ownership that Louisa became a village. With the sale of three acres of land to Willis and Levy, a thriving business district began.

On January 26, 1819, Henry Lawrence and his wife Mary sold to Charles Thompson Jr. and John M. Price the title to 392.5 acres of the courthouse tract for $25,000.[48] Excepted were the 2 acres belonging to Willis, the 1 acre belonging to Levy and 2 acres belonging to the county. The jail lot is not mentioned in this transaction. Charles Thompson and John M. Price made few changes during their ownership, but the changes they did make were of considerable importance—the sale of land to the railroad line to establish the Louisa Railroad and a depot in the village, for instance. The tracks ran on the northern edge of the village and the depot was located one block from the courthouse. Evidently, John M. Price lived at the courthouse and he became the postmaster for Louisa in 1818. He served until 1827.[49] In 1825, he obtained a license for operating a tavern, demonstrating that he lived at the courthouse for several years.[50] Like prior owners, he was also the local jailor.[51] John Marshall Price was born at his family home, Cool Water, in Hanover County in 1797. He was the son of Thomas Price and Barbara Winston. John Price married Elizabeth Carr Mosby and several of his children were born at Louisa Courthouse.

Thompson and Price sold to Leo Bullock one parcel of land upon which the old courthouse stood on January 29, 1821.[52] This is the land on which the Ogg building now stands. Thompson and Price continued the restrictions established by Lawrence on the land they sold. James H. Ellis owned this same one-acre lot for two years, from 1827 to 1829. Price and Thompson later regained ownership in 1829.[53]

An indication of the growth of the village was the building of Upper Gold Mine Baptist Church. Though not a part of the village at the time of its erection, it was certainly located in what is now the town of Louisa and within two blocks of Main Street. The best indication of its location is a description of the sale of two acres of land by Waddy Lipscomb to Roscal Rollow in March of 1824. The land is said to have been as "a little above the branch between said Lipscomb's tavern and the meeting House running along the line of Price Thompson to the meeting house spring."[54] This places Upper Gold Mine Church somewhere along Patrick Henry Drive between Church Avenue and Cutler Avenue. The land is beyond the senior ball field, which is behind the present town hall and at the end of Church Avenue. In 1830, David Hunter bought from Barret White 259 square poles upon which the meetinghouse called "Upper Gold Mine Church is situated."[55] One third went to William Stout on the western side of the lot. William Stout was the courthouse postmaster from 1828 to 1845.

The construction of the church is a good indication that the Baptist presence was stronger than other religions in the courthouse area. It also means that the church was there before 1824 and indicates that there were enough parishioners in the area to justify the building of the church. In Louisa's resolutions upon the death of Thomas Jefferson (on July 4, 1826), religious freedom is emphasized. The resolutions can be found in the Louisa County Minute Book. This resolution also emphasizes the feelings of the justices at the time.

Main Street, Louisa, circa 1911—Bonavita's Store stood on the tract where the second courthouse stood. The store (with the porch) is on the left. The windmill on the edge of the courthouse lawn dates the picture to circa 1911. *Courtesy of the author.*

> *The court and bar of this county, greatly deplore in common with their fellow citizens throughout the union the death of Thomas Jefferson, the patriot, statesman and friend of mankind his patriotism and pure republican principles as firm and unshakable as the mountain upon which he lived will continue to be remembered and fondly cherished from generation to generation throughout this wide extended confederacy, so long as liberty and the equal rights of man shall have votaries, he closed his mortal cause on the anniversary of that glorious day so dear as the author of the declaration made to the nations of the world that the united states was free and independent, as a statesman and philosopher he stood first among the foremost, his ardent soul strongly inspired at an early age with the equal rights of his countrymen in church and state, was amongst the foremost in advocating a separation of the two previously considered inseparable and permitting man to worship his creator in his own way, to him Virginia is indebted as the author of the bill for religious freedom which of itself would have immortalized his name. He was likewise one of the Committee of revisers who prepared a code of laws, afterwards adopted by the Virginia Assembly which abrogated the aristocratic features of the common law: but why enumerate his many useful services to*

John Hunter was clerk of Louisa County Court from 1820 to 1852. No limits were put on the county clerk's buying of land. He retained his holdings in the town for some time. Duncan Smith painted the portrait. *Courtesy of the Louisa County Circuit Court Clerk's Office.*

> *his country through a long period of sixty years: The first page of history already recorded when together with those of his compatriots and they will be perpetuated to the latest posterity: Resolved therefore unanimously together the courthouse and bar of Louisa County with its officers will wear crape* [sic] *for thirty days as a testimony of veneration and respect for the character of Thomas Jefferson.*[56]

In October of 1826, the Louisa Order Book reports a commissioners' report after an inspection of the jail.

> *There are three rooms to the jail, two in the second story each 16 by 14 feet and eight feet pitch for criminals and one in the first story 15 by 14 feet and 10 feet pitch for the confinement of debtors. The western room above wants 5 pains* [sic] *of glass in the windows and the iron facing on one window broken. There are 6 planks torn up from the floor and a gap of 2 & ½ feet high and 1 foot wide is made in the wooden lining of the wall. There is also a gap 2 or 3 feet long and 6 inches wide in another part of the said lining rendering this room on the whole not safe for custody. The eastern room above in which (Thomas Rutherford is now confined) is destitute of a stove or any means whatsoever of affording fire to warm the prisoner and has not been swept except by himself since his confinement there. The floor in consequence is not so clean as might be wished, in other respects the room is in neat condition. A plank of the lining is much decayed so as to be easily removed and leave the brick wall exposed, a part of the floor is also too much decayed, and 4 pains of glass are wanting in the windows. The debtor's apartment unoccupied at present wants one pain*[…] *The debtor's room has no locks as far as we could ascertain. We find that the jailor has been accustomed to find sufficient and wholesome food to Rutherford the only prisoner, now confined, except during one or two days when he was supplied only once a day. But the prisoner expresses himself satisfied with his general treatment.*[57]

This assessment of the jail and the jailor was part of the county's responsibility. The satisfactory jailor is John M. Price.

In 1832, Commonwealth's Attorney Lucien Minor proposed to build a lawyer's office on a twenty-foot square of public ground.[58] Lucien Minor, age forty-eight, was a prominent lawyer who worked at the courthouse for many years. He later edited the local newspaper and was a professor at the College of William and Mary, his alma mater. The law office was approved and built the next year. This makes what is now called the Crank Building the oldest known building now standing in the town of Louisa.

In 1833, John Hunter replaced John M. Price as co-owner of the courthouse property along with Charles Thompson.[59] John Hunter was clerk of Louisa County Court. He owned a good amount of land in the town and county.

Chapter 7

Joseph Martin's Gazetteer and the Railroad

Joseph Martin's gazetteer, published in 1835, provides an in-depth look at Louisa County. According to Mr. Martin, Louisa County in 1835 contained about 1,400 dwellings, ignoring those occupied by slaves. Most dwellings were one story and wooden, either framed or made of logs. Scarcely 20 were made of brick and painting was rare. In these houses lived 6,468 whites. The black population was listed as 9,382 slaves and 301 free blacks. The total population was listed as 16,151. Prosperous members of the population owned 3,036 horses, with 76 coaches, 44 carryalls and 91 gigs for transportation. The description of housing in Louisa County would also apply to the village. The village consisted of frame buildings, with the exceptions being the county offices, the courthouse, the clerk's office, the law office and the jail, all of which were built of brick. The conditions of the roads made it difficult to bring in supplies. It was necessary to build a kiln near the construction site in order to build with brick. Such things as nails and glass would be hard to come by until the train came through Louisa.

The 1835 list of professions and businesses in Louisa County included fifteen physicians, four lawyers, twelve ministers of the gospel, four saddler shops, fourteen tanneries, three carriage maker shops, five tailor shops, one silversmith, thirty gristmills (wheat), "machines for picking cotton and carding wool" and twenty stores where merchandise was sold.

Other towns, post offices and villages listed by Mr. Martin included Boswellville, Bradleysville, Cuckooville, Dabney's Mills, Gardner's Crossroads, Jackson, Locust Creek, Louisa C.H., Mechanicksville, Newark, Pottiesville, Thompson's Crossroads, Poindexter's Store and Yanceysville. Most of these areas contained little more than a country store and a post office.

The village of Louisa contained the following according to Martin's gazetteer: besides the courthouse and jail, there was a large house of worship, four stores, a silversmith, blacksmith, two carriage makers, two tailors, a shoemaker, a cabinetmaker, saddler, two taverns, a milliner, two lawyers' offices and a physician. According to Martin, the town held half the attorneys, the only silversmith, two of the five tailors and two of the three carriage makers found in the entire county. All twelve ministers in the county had

Early twentieth-century picture of the south side of Main Street. This is where the first business section in the town began. *Courtesy of Mrs. Aubrey Seay.*

occupations other than their ministry. The gazetteer also proves that there was a village of some consequence at the courthouse. The "large house of worship" could be Upper Gold Mine Church, but its location was considered out of the village of Louisa. More likely it was the Methodist church. There is positive record that the Methodist church building was there in 1840. It is not inconceivable that it was built five years earlier. With two taverns listed, it is unknown which was the original.

In order to bring some of these statistics to life, the following are some of the people who lived at the courthouse in the 1830s.

One of the tailors working at the courthouse was John H. Rosson. John Miles was the other. Mr. Rosson lived at the courthouse from 1835 to 1860. He first worked in a brick building that was part of the tavern property for about a year; next he worked in a building that was thought to be built by Elisha Melton. It was located between the new courthouse's wall and the old courthouse. He exchanged this house with John Poindexter. Mr. Poindexter wanted a law office closer to the tavern.[60]

Samuel P. Hackett was born in 1818 and lived at Louisa Courthouse from 1835 to 1840, and returned in 1871. He was a general businessman, magistrate, mayor of Louisa, newspaper editor and renter at Louisa. His first job was as a clerk in the store of Jones and Winston in Louisa.[61]

Robert Merideth Kent came to live in Louisa in 1835. He was a clerk for John Todd Quarles and later a partner with him. John Todd Quarles lived at Liberty Hall. In 1862, Robert Kent bought land south of the courthouse and built his home, Kalona.[62]

A.M. Trice lived at the courthouse for eighteen years. He came in the fall of 1831 or 1832 and learned his trade in the old courthouse building.[63]

Thomas B. Humphrey came to Louisa Courthouse in 1831 and stayed until the early forties. He advertised in the *Enquirer* on March 24, 1831, as a clock and watchmaker and a jeweler.[64] He later moved to Richmond.

Francis W. Jones advertised his dry goods business, which he claimed began in 1835.[65] He and his family remained in Louisa for many years.

By 1835, the dissenters had venotry certainly taken over the religious community: listed were 2,960 professing Christians; 1,450 Baptists; 1,340 Methodists; 140 Reformed Baptists; 20 Presbyterians; and 10 Episcopalians. Religion was practiced in twenty-five houses of worship.

Joseph Martin stated that the people of Louisa County were of moral and industrial habits, clothing themselves and their equipage with simplicity. Thirteen temperance societies existed, with about 1,200 members. There was also a Female Colonization Society, and several Bible, Tract, Missionary and Sunday School Societies.

In 1917, the National Bank replaced an old shop on the courthouse grounds, in the same location as the second courthouse, located on the second courthouse lot. It is believed that parts of the second courthouse were used in the building of the shop. Liberty Hall can be seen in the background. *Courtesy of the Griswold Boxley Collection.*

"Old field schools" were prevalent during the early 1800s in Louisa County. These schools were usually set up by community members in order to educate their children. The old field schools accepted poor children and were paid for by the county from a literary fund that was created in 1810 for poor children. There was one permanent classical school and several for plainer branches of learning. There were three female boarding schools. On average, five students were sent annually to the University of Virginia for higher education.

These schools did not include blacks due to a state law passed in 1831 that forbade assemblies for the education of blacks. More than a generation of blacks went without education in schoolhouses. Earlier, in 1819, fear of insurrection had engendered the registration of free blacks.

A major change in Louisa County came with the advent of the railroad. In May of 1836, the Louisa Railroad Company was formed by Louisa County men and became the first east–west railroad in Virginia. The company was organized with Frederick Harris of Fredericks Hall as president and J.N. Hopkins and James Hunter as engineers. The purpose of the train was to supply the landlocked Piedmont with transportation. The railroad facilitated travel and trade in Louisa, connected stage lines running through Charlottesville and Gordonsville and provided a new means of investment and occupation for a predominantly rural people.

A large depot at Fredericks Hall was the first terminal for the Louisa Railroad. The station was important as a terminal and a departure point for stage and private conveyance heading westward. Many of the wealthy took this route to the springs, where they spent their summer months. The railroad project was supported by the people of Louisa as it gave them employment.

A letter in 1837 gives us a feeling for the times:

> *He* [Colonel John Claybrooke] *has undertaken to get timbers for the railroad company which occupies nearly the whole of his time indeed all the gentlemen in the neighborhood are busily engaged. The whole vicinity seems to be in a commotion (men women and children) the ladies have to provide or at least to prepare the diet for the laborers (which by this time you know) is a delightful part.*[66]

The opening of the railroad was described in 1837:

> *We had our Christmas before the 25th, the opening of the Louisa railroad was the commencement which took place on 20th of December. The cars arrived at Fredericks hall depot 1 o'clock. It was a grand display three long coaches each containing passengers came up. They had a band of music and the American colors flying. It was a sight worth seeing, many hundreds attended, the road was lined with spectators, a proud day for Louisa was echoed from all quarters, who would have believed this ten years ago. Huza for old Louisa.*[67]

By December 1838, the railroad reached Louisa Courthouse, and by 1840, it extended all the way to Gordonsville. Louisa, after the construction of the line, increased

The logo for the 125th anniversary of the town of Louisa created an interpretation of the first train to travel through Louisa. First called the Louisa Railroad, the name was changed to the Virginia Central in 1850, when the line extended to the Jackson River, ten miles west of Covington.

in population by 12 percent from 1830 to 1860, and also developed economically. The actual train that traveled through Louisa would have resembled a stagecoach on rails.

When the railroad extended to Louisa Courthouse, there was a celebration in the village. The right of way through the courthouse tract was sold by Charles Thompson and John Hunter in 1836. The one individual exception was the right of way sold by Alexander Levy, whose land extended across the railroad tracts in 1838. The Louisa Courthouse Depot would make a huge difference in accessibility to Louisa Courthouse. One result of the railroad extension was the visit of the president of the United States to Louisa Courthouse in July of 1838. The courthouse depot was not ready for operation until December of 1838. In July, the president may have only passed through the courthouse after disembarking at another point. Louisa was where vacationers met the stage before continuing on to other destinations. The following was posted in the July 21, 1938 *Central Virginian*:

> *President Van Buren left Washington D.C. for the Richmond Rail Road to come to the Louisa terminal Rail Road. There he was met by his carriage from the White House which carried him to White Sulphur Springs. His wife and younger son accompanied him. Also with him was the Secretary of Navy and novelist James K. Spaulding. Mr. H. Fairfax Spaulding sent article.*[68]

Not everyone took advantage of the railroad. John E. Massey, a Baptist preacher, lawyer and lieutenant governor of Virginia, spent time in Louisa. He attended Dr. Gillispie's school in Louisa County and later taught in Louisa. He studied law under Starke W. Morris Esq. of Louisa Courthouse. In order to pay for law school books, he made spinning wheels and chairs in his father's shop in Spotsylvania and brought them to Louisa Courthouse and Spotsylvania Courthouse on court days via a horse cart.[69]

Dr. William A. Gillespie's School was located at Louisa Courthouse from 1839 to the early 1850s. His classical school was advertised at thirty dollars for a ten-month session, with board at eighty dollars. English, math, chemistry, natural philosophy and astronomy were offered at this "classical school" held at Louisa Courthouse.[70]

Chapter 8
Elisha Melton and the Churches of Louisa

On November 9, 1840, Charles Thompson and his wife, Sarah A., sold their part of the courthouse tract to Elisha Melton for $12,750. Elisha Melton was born January 18, 1800, the son of Thomas and Lydia Melton. Elisha Melton married Ann (Nancy) Tisdale Chiles in 1821. She was the daughter of John and Mary Tisdale Chiles. The Meltons lived at McGehees, south of Louisa Courthouse, and they are buried there. Elisha Melton died on September 17, 1854, of "king alcohol."[71] During his lifetime, he accumulated a great deal of property in Louisa County apart from the courthouse. He was owner of the courthouse tract for fourteen years. His main contribution to the growth of the town was the building of churches.

One exception to Melton's purchase of the courthouse tract was a small parcel given by Charles Thompson and John Hunter (who purchased John M. Price's parcel in 1833) to the Methodist Church for the purpose of building a meetinghouse. The building "has been built and is on the road leading by the said Courthouse."[72] The Methodist church, at that time, was a frame building on a triangular plot of land between Fredericksburg Avenue and Church Avenue, east of the depot. This frame building later became the first church for blacks in the village after the War Between the States. It is possible that this church was built before 1835 and was the "meeting house" listed in Martin's gazetteer. The Methodist Church appointed circuit riders beginning in 1835. Although listed in 1835 as only having ten members, the Episcopalians attempted to build a church at the courthouse in 1839.[73] The movement to build a church failed; however, the effort indicates that the village was growing.

On July 10, 1841, Elisha Melton bought John Hunter's half of the courthouse tract.[74] Included in the deed was one half of the furniture in the tavern. Elisha Melton became the sole owner of the courthouse tract. He owned vast tracts of land in Louisa County.

Robert Gooch, Hugh Cullen (silversmith) and Samuel Grymes (shoemaker) worked together about 1844 in the old courthouse, which was outside of the original fence.[75] Mr. Perkins had a grocery store on the corner.[76] Shopping in 1844 was much different than today—a store would more likely be filled with men than women. Servants or the man of the family did the shopping. In one month on record in a shop at the courthouse, 126 men bought items for themselves, 14 servants bought items and only 10 women came in the shop.[77] Most items were put on the tab with cash only used occasionally.

A change in the public county square was the addition of a brick wall enclosure. The county commissioners proposed to build a permanent brick wall around the courthouse in June of 1844.[78] This wall was built and replaced the wooden rail fence.

Robert T. Gooch came to live in Louisa about 1846 and maintained several businesses at the courthouse.[79] He bought the lot on the south side of Main Street next to John T. Quarles; it was originally the Willis lot of 1816.[80] It was here that he resided with his wife Martha S. Toler and worked as a merchant. Robert had lived in Tolerville (later Mineral) until his move to Louisa in 1846. He had established the Tolersville Post Office in 1837 and worked as postmaster until 1845 and also as a tavern keeper. Before that time, it is believed that he worked at a tannery in Tolersville. Once he moved to Louisa, he bought a half-acre lot on what was known as the Tan Yard branch of Beaver Creek, where he set up his own tan yard.[81] Today, this is the area across Elm Street from the nursing home. Robert Gooch also worked in the Louisa Post Office from 1848 to 1858.

An excellent source for determining the residents of the courthouse area are the rosters of Day Lodge No. 58, Ancient, Free and Accepted Masons, which was first chartered in 1799. It was chartered again on December 15, 1841.[82] James D. Cube was the first worshipful master in 1841.[83] Later housed above the Methodist church, the Masonic members may have met at the earlier Methodist church or at the courthouse. The rosters of the Masonic Lodge No. 58 list some of the people living at Louisa Courthouse in the 1850s. Leon Levy, son of Alexander, became a Mason in 1850. Later Masonic members include B.H. Priddy, who became a member in 1852 and was a coach maker at Louisa Courthouse; Charles F. Hudson, a tailor, 1853; William F. Cox, a tailor, 1855; and Samuel Grymes, a shoemaker, 1856. William H. Mills, a carriage maker, and Joe S. Hester, a tailor, worked and probably lived at the courthouse at some time.

Elisha Melton advertised his "Classical and Mathematical School" in 1849. Though it was one mile from the courthouse, it was associated with the courthouse and was one of Elisha Melton's many endeavors. The school taught English, Latin, Greek, French, Spanish, German and mathematics. Dr. A. McKee was the teacher, and board and tuition were $115 for ten months.[84]

Elisha Melton donated land to the congregation of Upper Gold Mine Church in June of 1849. The congregation was made up of 223 souls, black and white. The land assigned to the church was just across from the courthouse on the eastern side. Upper Gold Mine Church was organized in 1829 or earlier. The congregation of Upper Gold Mine constructed a more permanent building after 1849. The name was changed to the Louisa Baptist Church in 1885. Church membership was reorganized and renamed the Memorial Baptist Church in 1969.

Also in June of 1849, Elisha Melton sold land to the Disciples of Christ (now known as the Christian Church) for five dollars and other considerations. This was located behind the courthouse. James Gross, the first minister of the Disciples of Christ, began preaching in the courthouse until the church could be built. On January 26, 1851, the Louisa Christian Church was organized—it was about this time that their

Louisa Baptist Church. *Courtesy of Mrs. Aubrey Seay.*

brick church was built south of the courthouse. This church has been remodeled since its origin. It has a quaint cemetery adjoining it that is the only church cemetery in the town. In 1905, the vestibule and gallery were erected by the Ladies Aid Society in memory of Mrs. Bessie Gooch.

The Louisa United Methodist Church trustees bought land in June of 1852 and built the Louisa Methodist Episcopal Church with a second story for the Masonic Day Lodge No. 58. The Episcopalians were allowed to use the church one Sunday each month. This church originally had a small cemetery that was later moved. The Methodists already had a church—they may not have felt the need for a move, even of one block, until that time.

The process of reconstructing the village during the time the churches were being built is aided by the 1850 census. This census reveals numerous residents in the tavern, or hotel. There were twenty-three single men and four families. The hotel must have been fairly large to accommodate so many people, even with some of them sharing rooms. Most of the single men were younger than thirty years old, living at the only bar in town. Saturday nights can be imagined. The landlord, Jesse Melton (twenty-eight years old), was the nephew of Elisha Melton and in time became a contractor and built many Louisa homes during the 1860s. Thomas Walton was an assistant hotel keeper who resided in the hotel with his wife Isabella and their son William F. Walton. Four tailors lived at the hotel in 1850. John H. Rosson (twenty-eight years old) was the only tailor who had been at the courthouse for many years. His business was located next to the jail on the north side of Main Street. Three lawyers resided at the hotel: James L. Gordon (thirty-three), Edward H. Lane (twenty-five) and Henry W. Murray (twenty-three). They would occasionally be joined by other lawyers who had business at the courthouse. Two teenagers, William H. Carrick (fifteen) and William Cox (fourteen) were listed—they were certainly apprentices.[85] Construction was going on in the area because two painters and two carpenters were listed. Painter William Gunnell and carpenter Alfred Kennon are known local names. The oldest carpenter, James O. Carrol (thirty-five), lived at the hotel with his wife Sarah and two children, Virgil and Clara. The Carrol family later moved to a house on East Main, which is today the Brookman home. Hugh M. Cullen (thirty-three) was a watchmaker who lived at the hotel with his wife Mary Ann and three children, William, James and Edward. The Cullen family came in 1844 and later moved to the end of Church Avenue, which was then Depot Street. Watches and clocks were, at the time, considered extravagant and were taxed by the county. Alexis Netherland (thirty-one) was an assistant on the railroad; his wife Permelia, daughter Fannie and mother Ann were living with him. Jacob Manning (thirty-four), a Methodist clergyman, had a room with his wife Frances E. and his children, Elizabeth and Willie A. Manning. The Methodist ministers served a circuit of seven churches in Louisa County; the hotel must have been his home base as he was minister for only a year in Louisa. Because of their schedule, Methodist ministers were not encouraged to marry. Thomas S. Baker (twenty-one) was the lone student staying at the hotel.

The tradesmen and merchants must have worked in nearby stores and shops. Since the land was still privately owned, clues such as this must be used to consider how many houses and stores were in the village at the time. The earliest homes and stores were across from the courthouse and located on both sides of Elm Street. The courthouse tract was becoming known as the tavern tract. Other homeowners also resided at the courthouse.

Early transportation was taken care of by two harness makers, five carriage makers and two blacksmiths. Property taxes of the time listed four-wheel pleasure carriages, carryalls and two-wheel pleasure carriages as taxable property.

Frances E. Thompson, her three children and her mother, Mrs. Margaret Poindexter, lived on the corner of Elm Street and Route 208. They bought one and a half acres of land and the house in 1859 from John Cammack, but they were already living there. The architecture of the house indicates that it was built much earlier. Frances was the widow of Nathanial Thompson and the daughter of the influential clerk of court, John Poindexter. Frances lived in the house until her death in 1881.

Living at Liberty Hall on Elm Street, close to the corner of Main Street, was Francis W. Jones (thirty-two), a merchant, married to Ann Pendleton Ashby. The couple had six children: Helen M., John W., Francis P., Philip E., Robert M. and Lucy M. Jones. Mr. Jones's store was near their home and Josephus W. Anderson was a clerk in his store.

William Stout (fifty-three) was an early inhabitant of the village and had at one time lived at Liberty Hall. He was an assistant iron master and had a large family with his wife Letitia. William Stout was involved in the iron-mining and manufacturing operations at the Victoria Furnace near Tolersville (later Mineral) with John Hunter Sr.

Francis Jones. *Courtesy of the Masonic Day Lodge No. 58, Ancient, Free & Accepted Mason.*

Liberty Hall, demolished in 1940, was a tangible connection to the past. Many people today still remember seeing it standing. Liberty Hall was built by either the Quarles family or the Willis family about 1825. *Courtesy of Jimmy Tallie.*

Edwin Smith's family stands in front of their home on Ellisville Drive. Mary Ann Walton Smith is seated and surrounded by her children. Dr. Walton Oregon Smith is standing. This home was later enclosed in brick by D. Wiley Anderson, the architect for the courthouse, by order of the Boxley family. *Courtesy of the author.*

Several local merchants composed the business district of the village. Robert T. Gooch has already been mentioned. He employed two clerks: Pleasant M. Harlan (twenty-six) and Ed W. Eggleston (twenty-five). This indicated a fairly large inventory. George W. Minor (eighteen) was an assistant tanner and probably worked at Gooch's tannery. Robert M. Kent (thirty-four) was another prominent local merchant. He would later build Kalona just outside of town. All this activity was confined to the south side of Main Street and extended out of town to the Gooch tannery at the end of Elm Street.

On north Main Street, the main business was that of Hyman Levy (thirty-five). He lived with his wife Mary and their son Leon. He ran one of the oldest businesses in the town, started by his father Alexander in 1816. Evidently, it was a thriving business at this time since he was worth $4,000. They were the Wal-Mart of the times, providing ready-made clothes, dry goods, hardware and groceries. Hyman grew up outside of town in his family home but lived at the courthouse at this time. Henry W. Quarles was a clerk. Adjacent to Hyman Levy's store was the county jail.

Mercer W. Quarles (twenty-two) was the local doctor. He was evidently just out of school as he is listed as a first-year medical student at the University of Virginia from 1847 to 1849.[86] Edwin Smith (thirty-nine) was the dentist in the area. Edwin Smith, by

1859, lived across the railroad tracks at the beginning of Ellisville Road. He lived west of the courthouse on land that had been owned by William Walton. Dr. Smith married William's daughter Mary Ann Walton in 1842, and they inherited the land from him.

William W. Beadles (sixty-two), his wife Elizabeth and their four children lived just outside of the courthouse area to the east, in a building that now houses the Tanyard Country Club. His family was one of the oldest in the area.

In an 1854 indenture, it was stated that Elisha Melton was in financial difficulty and the courthouse tract was described therein.[87] The deed listed a tavern house, sundry storehouses, dwelling houses, offices, shops and other houses. The Quarles lot and the Gooch lot were included in the land owned by Elisha Melton. One-fiftieth of an acre is described as that "on which the house at Louisa Courthouse, stands known as the Old Court House, and formerly used for that purpose."[88] This is where the Ogg building now stands.

Chapter 9

John Cammack and Approaching War

The village of Louisa really started to grow in the period just prior to, and after, the War Between the States. The courthouse tract of 390 to 400 acres remained almost intact during the fourteen-year ownership of Elisha Melton. His sale of land to the three churches was the main exception to his autonomy in the village. After his death in 1854, the courthouse tract was bought by a group of speculators. On April 12, 1854, the tract was sold to Peter W. Dudley, John C. Cammack, Joseph R. Madison, George W. Trice, David M. Hunter, William Henderson and William Chiles.[89] This group of men began the town's division into separate properties (rather than keeping the land private, they were interested in speculation). John C. Cammack was the major owner of the property central to the town and the tavern property. He bought out the shares of the other members over the years. By 1856, he owned most of the tract, with only small exceptions in those tracts owned by William F. Chiles and William Henderson. John Chew Cammack was from Spotsylvania County, the son of Robert and Elizabeth Chew Cammack of Andrew's tavern; he married Jane Pendleton in 1844.[90]

During the War Between the States, little property traded hands. Immediately after the war, there was a boom in the real estate business in the village of Louisa. Purchases of small lots for residential and business purposes extended beyond the railroad tracks into what was quaintly called the suburbs of the town of Louisa—this was any land beyond the two- or three-block area of Main Street. It was after this growth that the village of nearly 250 inhabitants truly became a town.

Before the war a few homes were built, but the village was still very small. A reconstruction of the area gives an idea of other additions at that time. In 1859, Gable Manor (later Rose Cottage) was built on Elm Street by Judge Edward H. Lane. This Gothic Revival home is attributed to the influence of two architects—Alexander Jackson Davis and Andrew Jackson Downing. The home was used as a hospital during the War Between the States. Edward H. Lane became the first judge of the newly created Louisa County Court in 1870; he built his law office about the same time as his house.[91] Right next to Mr. Lane's law office on Elm Street was the home of Cynthia and Susanna Jones. This vernacular home was built some time before the war.

John Chew Cammack. *Courtesy of the Louisa County Circuit Court Clerk's Office.*

Mrs. Mary Madison owned and occupied a house and lot on both sides of the main road running through the village in 1860. There was a blacksmith shop and two large carriage shops attached to her land, which was considered prime real estate.

On part of the tavern tract, across the tracks and opposite the depot, an original vernacular building was standing well before the war. This tract was owned by Jesse Melton, the nephew of Elisha.

With the growth of the village, the restrictions against selling spirits were evidently extended by John C. Cammack to include restrictions against boarding employees or students within the courthouse tract.

Evidence of this is found in the January 1861 release of Frank V. Winston from further restrictions.[92] The said restrictions were previously worded "to restrain or prohibit the said Winston, his heirs or assigns from having a boarding school or from boarding any person or person who might desire to attend or be attending school or in the neighborhood of Louisa Courthouse or from boarding any person or persons in their employment or connected with them in business or from boarding any relative or connection by blood or affinity upon any portion of the land conveyed."[93] Frank Winston was buying land in the area of Donnally Dale in Louisa. It is the only indication found of further restrictions on ownership of the land. It would be to Mr. Cammack's advantage that all students and workers in the area board at the hotel. The only school advertised at the time was the J.P. Thompson "Louisa Male Academy," where boys were prepared for the University of Virginia.[94] Though he was selling off land, Mr. Cammack continued to control the area commerce.

Chapter 10

War Comes to Louisa

William Marshall Ambler of Louisa County, a delegate to the Virginia legislature and to the Secession Convention, was the first member to sign the Virginia Ordinance of Secession.[95] This was passed on April 17, 1861.

"On the morning of April 17, 1861, as the Louisa Blues, a volunteer company, was drilling on the courthouse green at Louisa, a telegram from the Governor of the State ordered the company to be ready to leave for the front at sunset."[96] The resolution for secession had been passed. "By sunset the Blues and other local citizens were congregated at the railroad depot with a local minister when his prayer was interrupted by the shrill whistle of an approaching train. Momentarily the citizen-soldiers boarded and were bound for Harpers Ferry."[97] The company was mustered into service at Harpers Ferry. They became Company D of the Thirteenth Infantry. Company D was made up of many courthouse residents.

The following were members of Company D of the Thirteenth Infantry from the village:

1. Captain Henry W. Murray, a lawyer born in 1826 in Dublin, Ireland, was the recruiter at the courthouse. Elected to office, he was not reelected in the reorganization and dropped out in 1862. He filed for compensation from the Confederate government when Stonewall Jackson's troops camped on his property near Louisa Courthouse in June of 1862. The troops burned rails and grazed horses on his meadows. In 1864, he served as clerk of the military court for the Third Corps, Army of Northern Virginia. (Henry W. Murray recruited the following troops on April 17, 1861.[98] Included are those who worked or lived at the courthouse or nearby.)
2. Lieutenant Frank V. Winston rose to captain in 1862. He was elected to the House of Delegates 1863–1864 and 1864–1865.
3. Lieutenant William Wallace Bird was a lawyer who graduated from the University of Virginia and qualified at the Louisa Courthouse in 1860.[99]
4. Lieutenant John N. Hibbs was a carriage maker at the courthouse. He was captured in 1864.

5. Sergeant Hugh M. Cullen was a merchant, age approximately forty-four, and was honorably discharged in 1862.
6. Sergeant Jesse J. Porter was the deputy county court clerk. He was promoted to second lieutenant in 1862.
7. Sergeant Samuel H. Parsons, a deputy Louisa County clerk, was promoted to third lieutenant in 1862. He was wounded in 1864.
8. William F. Cox, a tailor, was elected color sergeant in 1862.
9. Richard W. Eddins, a clerk, was first corporal and elected sergeant in 1862.
10. Fendol Chiles, a medical student, was a second corporal and severely wounded at Gains Mill in June 27, 1862.
11. Granville Mason was third corporal.
12. John Biggars was fourth corporal.

Privates of Company D of the Thirteenth Infantry:

1. Archibald Arnet was captured in battle on September 19, 1864.
2. Horace Bibb was on special duty as quartermaster in May of 1861.
3. Joseph W. Baker, a physician, was later elected first sergeant.
4. Alfred Baker was detailed as an ambulance carrier.
5. Marcellus Beadles died at Louisa Courthouse on April 17, 1862, of typhoid fever.
6. James Baker was wounded on May 12, 1862.

William Bird encampment. William Wallace Bird was a lawyer at Louisa Courthouse in 1860. He joined the Thirteenth Virginia Infantry there and sketched some of his experiences during the war. *Courtesy of Mary Minor.*

7. James M. Beadles was later a Baptist Minister at Louisa Courthouse.
8. Thomas Butler.
9. David S. Butler.
10. Henry Francisco joined another command and was killed at Kernstown.
11. James J. Gooch was later discharged.
12. William M. Goodwin.
13. Philip Edloe Jones was mortally wounded on June 7, 1862.
14. Charles S. Jones was later discharged.
15. Thomas Johnson.
16. William I. Kennon, a merchant, was discharged in June 1862.
17. James M. Lipscomb.
18. Richard Marshall.
19. George E. Moore, a carriage painter, was slightly wounded on August 27, 1862. He was later sent to Philadelphia.
20. Jefferson Melton.
21. Alexander G. Maupin died in Charlottesville hospital on August 8, 1862, of typhoid fever.
22. Edward B. Nucholls died of fever on July 15, 1862.
23. Winston O. Payne was mortally wounded on June 30, 1864.
24. Philip N. Porter was ordinance sergeant in 1862.
25. Will C. Pettus was wounded at the Battle of Fredericksburg on December 13.
26. Thomas P. Perkins.
27. John Padget.
28. James G. Pettus.
29. Francis Perkins was killed at Winchester.
30. James Quarles.
31. John M. Thomas.
32. Dabney A. Trice was wounded in June 1862.
33. Robert A. Trice was killed in June 1862.
34. James L. Thomason.
35. Robert N. Thomasson.
36. John W. Timberlake.
37. Andrew F. Tate.
38. J.W. Timberlake.
39. John Trice.
40. Julian Terrell was a lieutenant in 1864.
41. James M. Trice.
42. George M Toombs.
43. John W. Valentine.
44. Sam M. Waggoner.
45. James E. Winston.

Part of this list was made in 1902 by Frank Winston, Philip Porter and Joseph Baker.

Later enlistments by people who were associated with the Louisa Courthouse:

1. Charles M. Whitlock, July 17 1862.
2. William S. Hughson, July 18, 1861.
3. James F. Carpenter.
4. Dr. R.L. Barret, mustered May 2, 1862, assigned as assistant surgeon.
5. W.C. Barret, mustered May 26, 1862.
6. James M. Bickers, mustered May 7, 1861.
7. Nicholas Johnson, a doctor from Roundabout.
8. Francis P. Jones, a student, was an aid to General A.P. Hill and was mortally wounded at Gettysburg.
9. John William Jones, chaplain, enlisted at Harpers Ferry.

Left in the village during the war were women, children and older gentlemen. The 1860 census accounts for some of the older members of the community: Hyman Levy at fifty years old, Francis W. Jones at forty-eight and Henry Westheimer, a German of forty, were all merchants in the village of Louisa at the time of the war. William Rianold, forty-five, was a clerk in the store in 1860. Robert M. Kent, forty-four, was listed as a farmer but was also a merchant. Edward H. Lane, thirty-two, was a lawyer, and David M. Hunter, fifty-seven, was clerk of court. David Hunter was responsible for saving most of the Louisa County court records. The Louisa County records are almost all intact today. John C. Cammack, at forty, was listed as a farmer, but he was owner of the courthouse tract and the hotel. Patrick H. Jones, forty-two, was the proprietor of the hotel.

The Louisa Railroad had done some building before the war. Although it was reported that the Louisa freight station needed to be replaced in 1854, a passenger station was built instead. Buildings for the "special accommodation of passengers" were provided at Louisa Courthouse and Trevilian Station in 1856. "Since the business of the company has been so much enlarged, it has become proper to incur some expense for promoting the greater comfort of passengers, and also of giving permanence and security to the road itself."[100] The railroad provided more than transportation. A.W. Talley, age thirty-three, was hired as a railroad agent and stayed on throughout the war; he lived just outside of town. Robert T. Jennings, age twenty-eight, was a conductor on the railroad. The Louisa Railroad changed its name to the Virginia Central Railroad in 1861. It remained the Virginia Central Railroad until the end of the war. As a source of transportation and communication in Virginia, it was a target for the Northern armies.

Even with a war going on, it was suggested in 1862 that the Louisa Depot structure was unsafe and should be replaced with a brick building.[101] That same year, an enemy incursion destroyed some buildings at the Fredericks Hall railroad station but spared the Fredericks Hall Depot because it was close to a private dwelling.[102] These events were unsettling news for Louisa Courthouse.

Carter Scott Anderson, a conductor on the "accommodation" trains during the war, tells of the following event at Louisa Courthouse; he did not date this story but it was likely to have happened in the year 1862:[103]

Carter Scott Anderson. *Courtesy of the author.*

We remained at Louisa Courthouse for several days, including one Sunday, and a memorable Sunday it was. Our trains lay east and west of Louisa, covering about four miles of main track. We had no rations, scarcely, and there were so many soldiers about that it was impossible to buy anything to eat. By twelve o'clock noon more than half of the railroad men were drunk. We drank during the war mostly new apple brandy, and it is a very hot and fiery dram. A great many of the soldiers and the subordinate officers had come to town too and gotten drunk, and it was the jolliest crowd at the depot you ever saw. All at once = squeel- squell! Loud long and distressingly, we heard an engine coming from Richmond. We could not understand what on earth it could be, as we had with us every engine we had. "It must be a Yankee engine pulling McClellan's troops," said everyone. It was soon found out, however, that some official had run the gauntlet from Richmond and had gotten a little RF&P engine that happened to be outside of Richmond, and a little coach, and was making his way to Charlottesville.

The urgent request came to us to move all of our trains far enough east of Louisa until she could turn out of the west end of the switch. But, "here's the rub!" More than half of us were drunk, every engine cold, nobody knew anything, nor had anybody seen sense enough to appreciate our situation that we got the trains far enough west to let the courier train in, and then about the same trials to get them back down below the Courthouse, so that the little courier train could get out the west end and go on to Charlottesville. It took the best part of the day to get the track clear. In the meantime, it took so long for us to get the track open that the messenger man had either gone to see some of the officers or was getting his dinner, so that all of the railroad men and thousands of idle soldiers had gathered around to examine, criticize and find out all about this crew and its errand. My engineer Whalley, was pretty drunk.

He went around and chinned the little engine, made a great many ridiculous remarks about her, and finally bet twenty dollars that he could hold the little engine with ten men and could thus prevent her moving until he said so. Knowing the importance of the occasion, I begged Whalley not to attempt such a thing, it was too serious, but the soldiers told him to go ahead. Somebody took the bet and Whalley selected his men.

Presently here came the messenger, got upon the coach and told his engineer, "Go to Charlottesville; minutes are hours!" About twenty strong men dropped their strength against the coach. "Chow chow chow chow, spow, spow spow!" went the little engine.

I feared every minute that I would hear a shot. The engineer made several vain trials and seeing his point gained, Whalley said, "Giver her a push, boys and let her go." And off she shot amid the loud cheers of the soldiers. It was the most ridiculous sight I ever witnessed.

On April 29, 1863, Union Major General Joseph Hooker, commander of the Army of the Potomac, sent General George Stoneman, with about 3,500 cavalrymen, across Kelly's Ford to wreak as much destruction as he could on the Virginia Central Railroad. General David McMurtrie Gregg's men arrived at Louisa Courthouse on the Virginia Central Railroad at 2:00 a.m. on May 2, 1863. Three of his columns began tearing up the tracks and telegraph lines, and others ravaged and wrecked the railroad yard and storerooms containing rations.[104] From Louisa Courthouse, they moved on to wreak havoc on other parts of Louisa.

In February of 1864, Union General Judson Kilpatrick dispatched Colonel Ulric Dahlgren with five hundred men toward the Virginia Central Railroad as part of a plan to conduct a raid on Richmond. Dahlgren's raid caused damage, but they did not reach Louisa Courthouse.

Chapter 11

The Battle of Trevilian Station

The Battle of Trevilian Station in Louisa was a cavalry fight, but most of it was fought by dismounted troopers with firepower, as usual, favoring the Union primarily because of their use of Spencer repeating rifles. On June 7, Major General Philip Sheridan, commander of Cavalry Corps, Army of the Potomac, with about eight thousand horsemen, left Grant's army at New Castle, crossed the North Anna River at Carpenter's Ford and moved into Louisa County by June 10, 1864. They bivouacked at Clayton's Store. Sheridan was to tear up the Virginia Central Railroad somewhere between Gordonsville and Louisa and cut off Lee's supply line to the valley.

Meanwhile, on June 8, 1864, Major General Wade Hampton, Confederate commander, Cavalry Corps, Army of Northern Virginia, was ordered by Lee to take his division and that of Major General Fitz Lee, numbering about five thousand cavalrymen, to interpose his command between Sheridan and the railroad. Hampton reached Louisa Courthouse by June 10 and camped with Brigadier General Thomas L. Rosser in the Green Springs area on the Gordonsville road as darkness closed in. Brigadier General M.C. Butler's brigade bivouacked around Trevilian Station with Colonel G.J. Wright's command on the east and Major General Fitz Lee on the east side of Louisa Courthouse.

Brisk fighting went on all the next day, with Hampton finally taking up a strong position several miles west of the railroad station while Fitz Lee was driven toward Louisa Courthouse. Blue and Gray forces swayed back and forth all day with the advantage going to one side and then the other; as the long day closed, the Union troops had the better of it. "Several hundred yards in front and northwest of the Court House on June 11, 1864, General Wade Hampton led the boys of 'The Cadet Company' in a charge through a railroad excavation that repelled Union cavalry that was attacking Hart's artillery battery."[105]

"The Confederates overhauled Sheridan at the Louisa Court House, on June 11, 1864, and there was a sharp fight between the head of our column and the rear of the enemy's."[106] They were able to stay the enemy until Rosser could attack their flank.

The next day, the Battle of Trevilian Station continued. Although the Battle of Brandy Station is recognized as the greatest cavalry battle of the war, with over 20,000 Union and Confederate troops engaged, there were fewer casualties than those suffered in the Battle of Trevilian Station. In the battles on June 11 and June 12, Sheridan lost 93 men and nine officers; 438 men and 32 officers were wounded; and 427 men and 8 officers were captured or missing—a total of 1,007 casualties.[107] An estimate of Hampton's losses reached 1,071.[108] Sheridan did not reach Charlottesville and only caused minor damage to the railroad.

Of the most severely wounded, 90 had to be left behind in three field hospitals; in its retreat from Trevilian Station, Sheridan's force was accompanied by 377 causalities and 370 prisoners, including 20 officers. His situation was critical. He was deep in enemy country and his ammunition reserves were almost exhausted. Conditions of both men and animals were poor and he had to feed 7,000 men as well as more than that number of horses. Moreover, hundreds of Negroes had attached themselves to his column. From Sunday onward, they came in ever-increasing numbers: men, women and children.

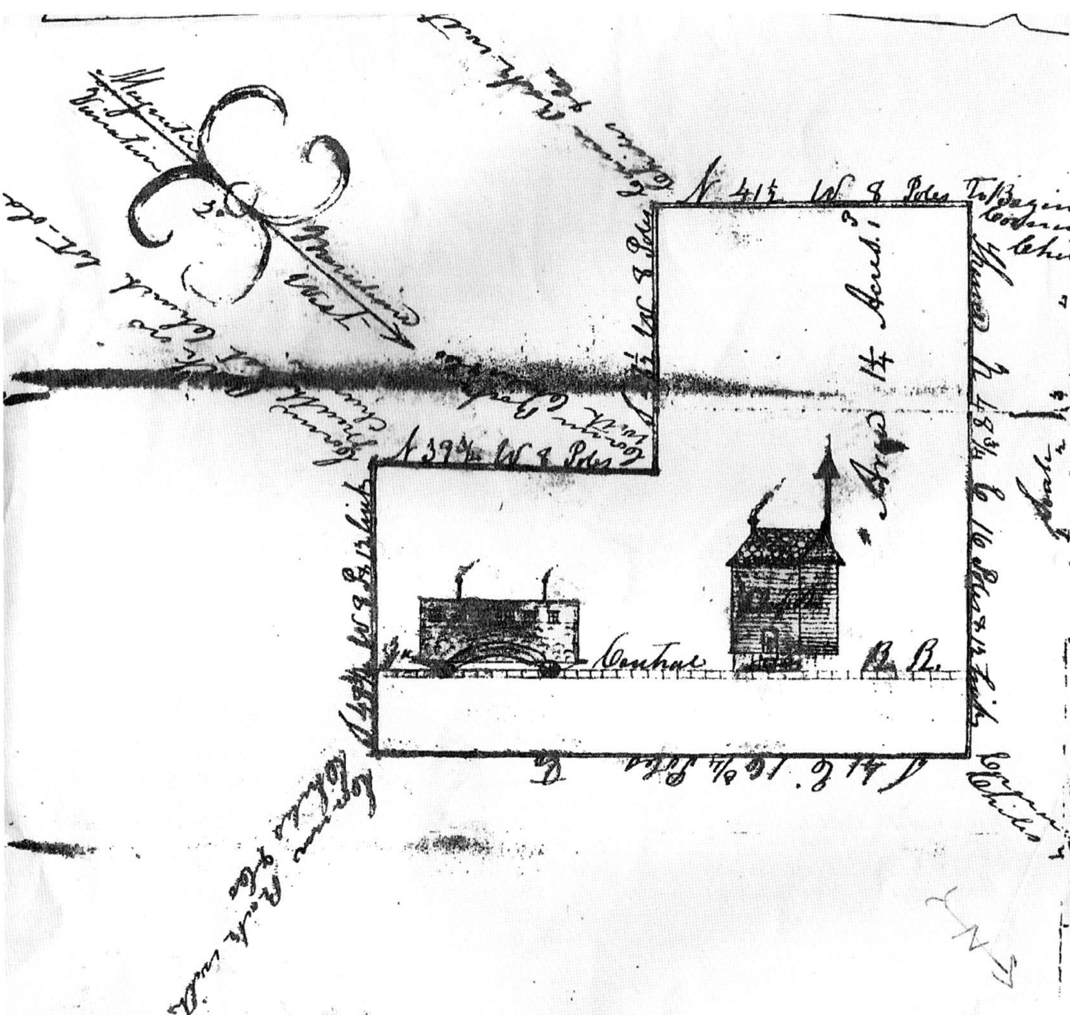

A plat for the railroad depot gives an artist's rendering of the earlier site, indicating a small depot during time of war. *Courtesy of the Louisa County Circuit Court Clerk's Office.*

Their worldly possessions were packed in pathetic little bundles that included little if any food. These people, too, had to be fed and their numbers soon reached 2,000.[109]

Sheridan also left a supply of medicines, liquor, hardtack, coffee and sugar. Assistant Surgeon Sickler of the Tenth New York and several attendants were caring for those left behind. Residents in the area treated all the wounded with tender care and all those who could be moved were brought to the railroad and taken to Gordonsville hospital in construction cars that had no springs and were open to the weather. The wounded, clad in blue and gray, waited patiently for the cars and were ministered to by women of the neighborhood, who brought with them whatever meager supplies and bandages were left to them. Aside from the field hospitals that had been set up, others were established at the Louisa railroad station, the tavern, the Louisa Methodist Church and the Old Courthouse in Louisa. Ties were cut, new rails were laid and eleven days later, on June 24, the railroad was open again for traffic.[110]

At Louisa Courthouse, Oakland Cemetery was established as grave after grave was dug and ninety-four nameless bodies of Union and Confederate soldiers were placed in graves—Americans all.[111] This beautiful cemetery created for the interment of soldiers fell into disrepair. In 1890, it was stated that "it is impossible to walk any of the paths without performing a Japanese salute, bending nearly to the ground owing to low-hanging boughs."[112] Oakland Cemetery fell into a state of further neglect after the town established Hill Crest Cemetery in 1935. Dr. Joseph W. Baker formed a cemetery board, made up of himself, W. Earle Crank and R. Lindsay Gordon, to restore the cemetery. By 1978, it was turned over to the Town of Louisa to ensure perpetual care. Among the distinguished citizens buried there are (in 1980) "about 100 Confederate and Union soldiers killed in the Battle of Trevilian Station, eight doctors, seven ministers, eight lawyers, two dentists, a county judge, two county sheriffs, three county clerks, two county treasurers, one Master of Virginia Masons, two mayors of the Town of Louisa, three proprietors of the old Louisa Hotel, two editors of the *Central Virginian*, a Louisa County hangman, and of course, four former members of the Virginia General Assembly."[113]

It was reported by the Virginia Central superintendent in 1865 that the Union army destroyed all the station houses east of Trevilian Station except for the depot at Fredericks Hall and "the passenger station at Louisa Courthouse, which were considerably injured in April of 1865."[114] The Louisa buildings mentioned remained in poor condition and were not replaced until 1868.[115]

Chapter 12
Aftermath of War

Rule by Federal troops and harsh Reconstruction policies following the war left the South in despair and delayed both reunification efforts and amicable relations. Louisa faced hard times but rebuilt its county little by little.

The clerk of Louisa County Court, David Morris Hunter, served out his two terms as the first clerk elected by popular vote. In 1865, John C. Cammack stepped into the post of county clerk. David Hunter turned the courthouse over to John Cammack in good condition. Hunter's deputies, Jesse J. Porter and Samuel H. Parsons, were both commissioned officers during the war and were not allowed to take Hunter's position. John C. Cammack appointed Mr. Porter and Mr. Parsons as his deputies in 1866. John Cammack was in a position of power in the town and county. He was busy selling his land in the town and was integral to the sale of land in the county. John Cammack remained in the position of Louisa County clerk until 1869, when General George Stoneman, commanding the First Military District in the state of Virginia, appointed William W. McGehee clerk of court.[116] William McGehee appointed John Cammack, Jesse Porter and Samuel Parsons his deputies. William McGehee served one year. In 1870, Mr. Parsons and Mr. Porter were appointed Louisa County clerks under a new constitution. Mr. Porter became clerk of the county court and Mr. Porter clerk of the circuit court.

Major General Alvin Coe Voris was installed as the first military governor of the Albemarle Military District, which included Louisa under Reconstruction at the end of the Civil War.[117] When he left the area to return to Akron, Ohio, he received a special commendation from the people of the district because they felt they could not have had better treatment than had taken place under his leadership. Serving under Major General Voris were the Ohio Infantry Volunteers. It was an ethnic hodgepodge of troops that came to the courthouse. Company G of the Ohio Volunteer Infantry included members who were, of course, from Ohio but also from Holland, England, Germany, Ireland and other countries in Europe. One can imagine the inhabitants of the town dealing with the discordant accents of the soldiers established in their village.

Major General Voris's letters to his wife describe the district and Louisa during his occupation.

May 4, 1865
I have the district assigned to my command consisting of the west half of Henrico and Hanover counties, the whole of Goochland, Louisa, Fluvanna, and Albemarle. My duties are of an indefinite and multitudinous sort that embrace the promotion of order, protection of darkies; development of loyalty, etc., everything else. I start for the interior in the morning.[118]

Louisa Courthouse, Va., May 12, 1865
I am living in sight of the mountains sixty-five miles from Richmond in a beautiful but poor country. Tobacco culture, slave labor and the war have made what was once one of the finest countries in the world a very poor country indeed.[119]

To escape from a government that they supposed was used to do much for the free states and so little for them was made a high political virtue and many, very many believed they had good reasons for exciting discontents and urging revolution.

I thank God for myself and my children that I am not a slave owner. The burdens and disabilities it throws on the owner in Virginia never compensated the community for the costs even when the individual owner made it profitable, which cases are rare—

Honest thinking persons tell me that they have no doubt that Virginia is better without slavery than with it. But all feel as if at this time it is costing an almost insupportable burden on them. All are poor here now.

Persons with pockets full of what was used for money one year ago, are absolutely penniless. Those who have hundred of thousands of Confederate Government bonds are as poor as if they had the same weight in paper rags only, and the owners of real estate have few horses, no other kinds of farm stock, hardly grain enough to keep themselves and three Negroes from starvation, till after harvest and everything in the nature of home or domestic supplies are so battered and worn under the pressure of four years war and a searching blockade that all are compelled to begin almost anew.

The colored in many instances are as well off as the whites with the advantage of knowing how to work.[120]

The railroad is now open to this place, but it is so infirm that it is all a person's neck is worth to ride on it—[121]

(After the war, the Virginia Central Railroad was renamed the Chesapeake and Ohio Railroad. At this time, the railroads came under government regulation.)

Louisa Courthouse, Va., May 28, 1865
I am in a tent again, fixed up in grand style in the Court House Yard of Louisa Co. I have a board floor, good chairs and a clean grass plot for door yard.[122]

Louisa C. H., Va. May 30, 1865
I am seated in my tent all alone 8 1/2 p, with bright moon beams overhead and the song of the toad all around and otherwise quiet prevails except the song the cricket sings and the not very melodious efforts of a lady at her piano a few rods off. O! I forgot the matter of

> *the dishes at the room of the officers of my staff and the rattling of the town pump and the chatter of the darkies.*[123]

Around the town, Reconstruction brought new buildings to Louisa. Using plans submitted by W.L. Kuper, the jail was moved from the north side of Main Street and erected on the courthouse lawn in 1868. An inmate burned the wooden interior of the previous jail in an effort to escape. This method of escape was a recurring favorite. The county utilized the bricks and wrought iron from the earlier 1808 jail as well as adopted a similar architectural style.

Edmund P. Goodwin bought land in 1867 that was part of the original "Tavern tract." This land was located across from the depot. He built a vernacular "I"-shaped home for his wife, Lucy A. Goodwin, in 1868. The house remained in the Goodwin family until 1951. Lucy Goodwin was postmistress of the Louisa Court House Post Office from 1877 until 1889, when the name was changed to Louisa Post Office. George D.M. Hunter took over for her for one year in 1881. Part of her land was sold off in 1870 to build store buildings on Main Street, expanding the business district to the corner of Church Avenue.

After the war, the black population was very mobile—decisions had to be made whether to stay in a place they considered home or to leave for better prospects. In the village, the blacks who had belonged to the white churches in town separated and formed their own church. In 1866, the First Baptist Church of Louisa was officially organized by the Reverend Fountain Perkins. He was sent to this section of Virginia by a missionary group to assist black members in establishing churches.[124] The first pastor was the Reverend J.W. Barnett. The congregation met in the old Methodist church near the railroad station. This building was the original Methodist church built about 1840. Members of this church certainly welcomed a returning Louisa son when John Mercer Langston came to visit.

John Mercer Langston was born in Louisa County on December 14, 1829, "the child of my father's old age."[125] He was the fourth child of Captain Ralph Quarles (a white plantation owner) and Lucy Langston. Lucy Langston was a slave who was freed by her owner Ralph Quarles in 1806. After the death of Ralph Quarles and Lucy Langston in 1834, John's older brother Gideon felt it best that John be relocated to the free state of Ohio. John Mercer Langston grew up to become the first black American to be elected to public office (a post in an Ohio township) in 1855 and later served the Freedman's Bureau as inspector general. He was the first dean of the Howard University Law School, was named U.S. minister to Haiti in 1877 and was the first black person sent by Virginia to Congress to serve in the House of Representatives in 1890. He returned to Louisa for a visit after the war. On June 15, 1867, Mr. Langston reached Louisa Courthouse as inspector general of the Freedman's Bureau. He was inspecting the school systems throughout the South. This was the first visit to Louisa since he left in 1834. Mr. Langston was welcomed at the depot and taken to the Louisa Hotel. He addressed a large crowd of people, black and white, from the steps of the hotel. He was made welcome by one and all. The whites came to hear "Quarles's boy" and the blacks "Lucy's son." After his address to the crowd, he was invited to address a large group of women at the Baptist church. He spoke on "the Duty of the American Woman in This Hour of our Reconstruction."At the conclusion of his speech, William F. Gordon, commonwealth

Louisa Hotel. Though this is not the hotel where John Mercer Langston stood, it is in the approximate location. The hotel still stands and is now the Cooke Building. *Courtesy of the author.*

attorney of Louisa, delivered an endorsement of the address of the afternoon and the speech of the evening.[126]

John Mercer Langston was not the only orator to come to the courthouse. "In 1869, when negroes were first allowed the right of franchise, 'Henry Happy' Wells, the Carpet Bagger candidate for Governor addressed an immense concourse of black sovereigns from the stone steps that led from the street to the court green. It was a very warm day and the man who failed to be Virginia's Governor delivered his harangue under the shade of an umbrella held by a 'brother in black' whose grinning features betokened the high felt honor of his position[...]At the conclusion of Well's speech, Hon S. Wise appeared in one of the courthouse windows, and steadying himself on the sill by a hold on the blind with his left hand delivered one of the most impassioned political speeches that I have ever heard."[127] Politics of the time and for years to come were very personal in Virginia, and Louisa hosted many public speakers through the years.

In 1869, a new constitution was made for Virginia called the Underwood Constitution. The convention that shaped the new constitution consisted of a majority of representatives from the North and from foreign lands. In the minority were white Virginians, a total of 105 members.[128] Although this constitution framed by "aliens" was automatically scorned by the white population of Virginia, it implemented some needed reforms still in effect today. The Underwood Constitution remained in effect until 1902. It was under this constitution that a board of supervisors was created to preside over townships, which replaced districts. A superintendent of schools was also created by the new constitution. The free public school system for whites and blacks was established by the Underwood Constitution.

Chapter 13

From Village to Town

In 1870, the largest concentration of the county population was located around Louisa Courthouse. About 250 people lived in and around the courthouse. The town's history of establishing educational institutions parallels the county's.

The Reverend Mr. Littleberry J. Haley became the first superintendent of Louisa County Schools under the new constitution. The Reverend Mr. Haley, during his term of office (1872–1882), organized the present school system and set it in motion.[129] In his diary, Mr. Haley wrote, "I learn from all quarters that the people of Louisa County are violently opposed to the School Law and the whites generally will not vote an increase in taxes for school purposes."[130] Prior to this time, the only public schools were charity schools. The association was unfortunate. Nonetheless, progress was made by Mr. Haley. On May 25, 1872, a school levy was passed in Louisa County. The needed funds were raised by a levy of fifteen cents per one hundred dollars.[131]

By 1874, Littleberry Haley notes in his diary that he examined the following teachers at Louisa Courthouse: Robert E. Harris, W.T. Meade, Mrs. Hackett, Miss Sue Paine, F.L. Woolfolk and Mrs. Woolfolk, Carrie E. Melton (colored) and Misses Peake.[132] Though the county spent more time and money on education for whites, there was also education for blacks, even at this early date. From 1870 to 1906, black education was funded by churches, Northerners and philanthropists. Publicly funded education was meager for both black and white.

The first black school in the Louisa Courthouse District prior to the public school system had one teacher, Mrs. Shaw from New England. During this period, black citizens provided the building and the fuel for the school and boarded the teacher.[133]

In 1877, the first Louisa County Public School was built for white students. In 1876, land was bought for the new school on Elm Street; the school was built and the doors opened in 1877. The school was named Haley High after the Reverend Mr. Littleberry J. Haley. The first superintendent of schools for Louisa County, the Reverend Mr. Haley, did much for free education in Louisa. Haley High was a frame school, consisted of four classrooms and served Louisa and neighboring counties. Haley High was closed in 1907. In 1883, a training school for black students was built in the town of Louisa.

The first public high school in Louisa. *Courtesy of the* Central Virginian.

An act to incorporate the town of Louisa in Louisa County was approved on March 8, 1873, by the Virginia General Assembly.

> *Be it enacted by the General Assembly THAT the town of Louisa, in Louisa County, as the same has heretofore been or may hereafter be laid off in lots, streets and alley, shall be and the same is hereby made a town corporate, by the name of the Town of Louisa and by that name shall have and exercise the powers conferred on towns by the 54th chapter of the code of 1860, so far as the same is in force and shall be subject to and governed by all laws now in force or which may hereafter pass for the government of towns containing less than five thousand.*[134]

Under this act, a plat of the town was laid off, using trees, stables and yards as markers. A town council of seven trustees was chosen. The council was responsible for keeping the streets in order, paving roads and making necessary improvements with the power of taxation and passage of ordinances. A president of council was to be elected who would also serve as mayor with the power of a justice of the peace within the town. The mayor and town council were to be annually elected by qualified town voters. Also elected would be a town sergeant, who would serve as conservator of the peace. The town sergeant had the power to arrest all offenders within one mile of town limits and to collect taxes.

The first Louisa County Town Council consisted of George J. Sumner, Dr. Gulielmus Smith, Jesse W. Melton, Hyman Levy, Samuel H. Parsons, Henry W. Murray and

Francis W. Jones. At the first meeting, George J. Sumner was elected president, or mayor, and Samuel H. Parsons was elected secretary/treasurer by council members. Dr. Gulielmus Smith was a dentist from Spotsylvania who moved to Louisa after the war. He bought a house on the old tavern tract, across from the depot, from fellow councilman Jesse Melton. Dr. Smith added an office onto the house to get business from the train passengers. He lived and worked in the home, and his children left their names etched in the upper windows. Jesse W. Melton, the nephew of Elisha Melton, was a contractor who probably built most of the houses in the village before and after the war. He lived across the street from Dr. Smith on Depot Street (Church Avenue) on land that is today the fireman's field. His house has long been gone. Hyman Levy was the son of Alexander Levy, who bought the second piece of private land in the town in 1816. Mr. Levy may have lived above his store at some point. Samuel H. Parsons was a Louisa deputy and county clerk. He lived on East Main Street in the house known as the Lewise Cosby Home. Henry W. Murray was an Irishman who had practiced law in Louisa since 1849. He built his home next to the Louisa Methodist Church. Francis W. Jones owned and operated a dry goods store, established in 1835, across from the courthouse on Elm Street, and lived in "Liberty Hall." His son, John William Jones, a Baptist minister, was chaplain for the Confederate troops.

The most interesting personage was the new mayor, George J. Sumner, a grocer who moved to Louisa in 1866. He was born in Massachusetts. He lived in Richmond in 1850, before the war, but was too old to fight.

In size, the town was much smaller than today. To the east, the town line was located near the new police office; to the north, the line followed from a little above School Street to the edge of Sims Avenue to a white oak tree; to the west, the town line was located between West Street and Loving Street; and to the south, the line was parallel to the north side of the Tanyard Branch of Beaver Creek and near Thomasson's Funeral Home on West Street.

The main order of business for the new town council was the selection of a town sergeant and the drafting of the town bylaws. Both items were sent to committee. William A. Douglas was appointed as first town sergeant and served until June 1877, when he resigned.[135] He was also the county jailor. By March 28, 1873, town bylaws were presented to the town council by committee. Twenty-three ordinances were passed that began with a fine for speeding (by horse or vehicle) and ended with a tax on druggists. The two most unusual ordinances were that no person be allowed to permit their hog or hogs to run wild in the streets and that it was the duty of the town sergeant to remove all dead bodies and other such nuisances left within the limits of the town.

The early streets were bordered by plank walks and tan bark walks, with bridges built to cross over muddy ditches and steppingstones provided to cross the streets. Pens for stray pigs were built and horse racks were erected for those doing business in town. The water supply consisted of individual wells and a public well at the corner of the courthouse that was jointly owned by the town and county.

The town minutes give us an idea of the problems of the first years, but only in a minimal context. Communications in the town were greatly enhanced by the local

This picture of the courthouse (built in 1818) gives an excellent idea of the condition of the streets at the time. The picture was taken prior to 1905. *Courtesy of the Griswold Boxley Collection.*

newspaper. They gave a more rounded picture of the times. The first known newspaper was a sheet started in the late 1870s by William McKensie Bickers and written in longhand. Later, the *Louisa Weekly Record* was edited by Daniel Murphy and by W.M. Bickers. This newspaper ran for two years.[136]

In the *Louisa Record* in May of 1876, the following article was found; it illustrates the frustrations and uncertainty of the times.

> *Our post office seems destined, not only to be removed in regard of the office, but also in regard to the postmaster. It has been but a short while since Mr. Dunnington was removed and now Mr. Turner has been removed also, and Lasarus Bibb, colored, put in his place. What charges existed against Mr. Turner, we do not know—in fact, we doubt whether there were*

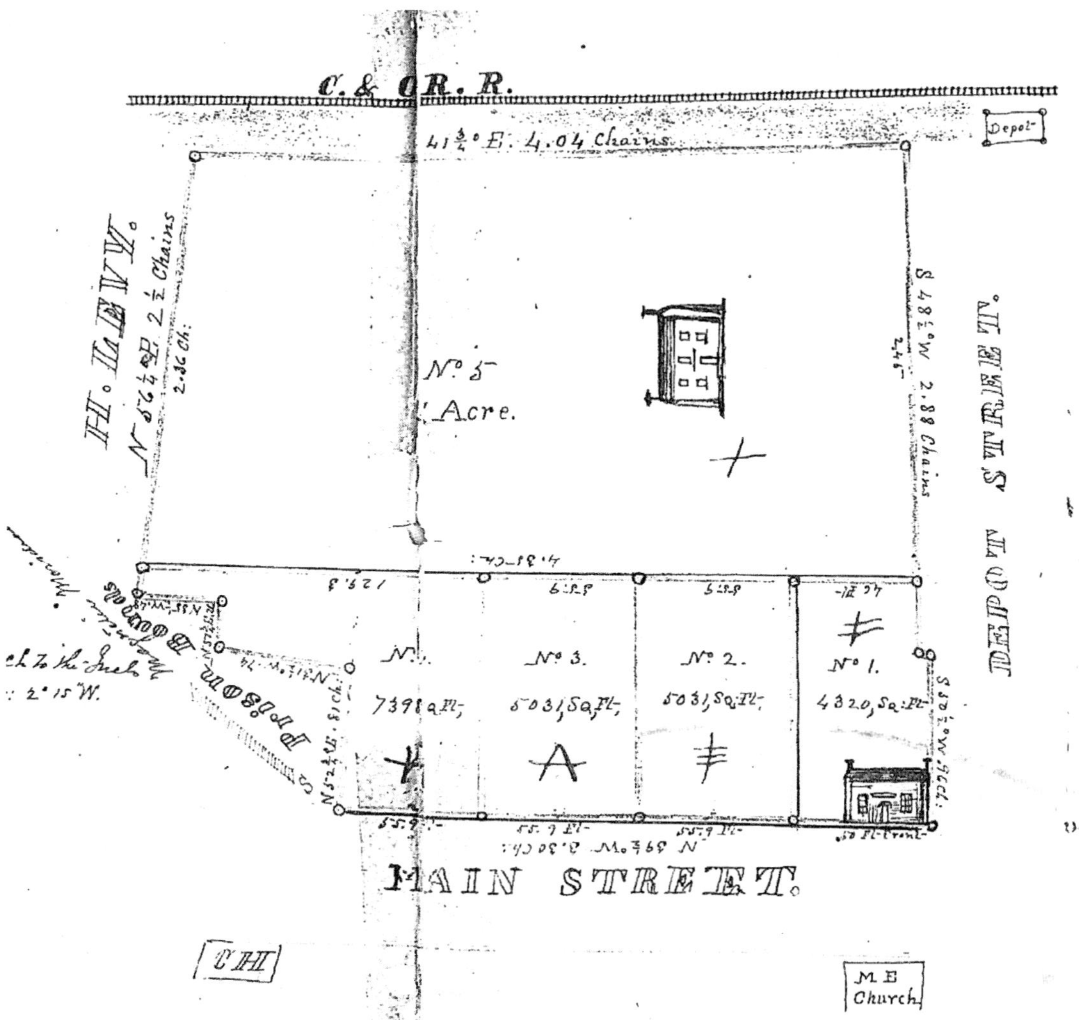

Map of the Goodwin property. By 1871, Mr. Goodwin sold his land on the corner of Church and Main Streets to Mr. W.O. Thomas. He adjoined the lots of S.D. Gooch, Young, Bickers and Mr. Smith. *Courtesy of the Louisa County Circuit Court Clerk's Office.*

> *any. This thing of removing an officer with out notification or specification of the cause is simply ridiculous. But who can expect more from such an administration? Mr. Turner is an accommodation gentleman and as postmaster, has we believe, given general satisfaction. We can for our part testify to his uniform courtesy in our intercourse with him.*

President Grant's administration was, at the time, under a cloud of suspicion of corruption. For a small town, interference by the government was the last thing desired. Lasarus Bibb was a grocer and merchant at Louisa Courthouse. He lived right on the eastern town line in what is today called the Deane House, also known as the Maddox House. George Turner was postmaster from November of 1875 to May of 1876. Lazarus Bibb lasted a full year, from May of 1876 to July of 1877, when he was replaced by Mrs. Lucy Goodwin, who was postmistress for many years. In this time of Reconstruction, it is interesting that the first black postmaster at the courthouse was followed by the first female postmistress.

On the lighter side, the *Louisa Weekly Record* also mentioned May Court Day in 1876. "Bustle was considerable, an agent for Dr. Hamilton's celebrated compound kept a noisy crowd around him all day—a wheel of fortune was displayed and kept running in the public street and a swindler held sway near the Hotel on a sleight of hand alias a roguery performance until he was compelled to stop by the way of arrest." Court days were still bringing in the people to the Louisa streets. The town also drew vendors from other areas and certainly medicine men.

View of the town of Louisa, looking west. *Courtesy of Mrs. Aubrey Seay.*

In 1878, the first streetlights, large oil lamps placed atop posts and twelve in number, were placed around town. Mr. W.H. Vaden made his rounds each morning with a small ladder; at each lamp, he would trim the wicks and clean the globes. He would light each lamp at dusk. The picture this creates provides us with a clear focus on the rural nature of the early town of Louisa and the progress that was yet to come.

Even with a new constitution, a new school system and new town taxes, not everything ran smoothly. The Louisa trustees' power was contested in 1878. B.F. Trice felt that the trustees acted out of order when they replaced member John C. Cammack Jr. with George Blubaugh. Mr. Cammack resigned after being out of town for several months and the council replaced him without an election. Additionally, Mr. Trice felt that the board of trustees had no authority to enact a capitation tax. This tax was passed with only Francis Jones, Henry Murray, Guilielmus Smith and Hyman Levy attending. It required two-thirds of the council to be present. Mr. Trice, the owner of the hotel, refused to pay his taxes because he felt the law was illegal and he had already paid his state and county taxes. Because he did not pay, the town sergeant auctioned off his mule and bay horse. Mr. Trice stated that he needed his horse and mule and that the sergeant

St. James Church: W.J. Whitlock, Anna Gris Boxley, Angie Whitlock, Agnes Whitlock, Mrs. Timberlake, Patricia Atkins, Milton Wayne Atkins, S. Edward Whitlock, Robert Whitlock, Linda Whitlock, Ethel Wythe Boxley, Kate Hatch and Jane Southard. *Courtesy of Ed Whitlock.*

First Baptist Church. *Courtesy of the* Central Virginian.

could have taken something from the bar for the taxes. It becomes clouded on whether he was fighting the taxation or the loss of his horse and mule. In the end, Mr. Trice retained his horse and mule through several technicalities. The town minutes from 1878 to 1882 do not exist so the town council's reaction is unknown.

The *Piedmont Free Press* was the local newspaper from 1879 to 1883.[137] The *Louisa County News* also ran from 1879 to 1903. The *Louisa County News* was first called the *Louisa News and Farmer* by James E. Bibb. He later changed the name in 1891. The paper was printed with an old Washington hand press. In 1903, Mr. Bibb sold the paper to R.W. Crawford, who changed the name to the *Louisa Goochland Enterprise.* Linda Henderson later edited this paper, followed by David N. Walker in 1905, who changed the title to the *Louisa Enterprise*. The paper later merged with the *Central Virginian*.[138]

Finally, after being disestablished after the Revolutionary War, the Episcopalians gained enough members and resources to build a frame church in 1881. With freedom of religion, the Anglican church lost its status as the state religion. After losing their church lands and many members, the recovery in Louisa was slow. St. James Episcopal Church was established largely through the efforts of Reverend James Grammar. It took another hundred years or so for St. James to receive full church status under the leadership of the Reverend John von Hemert in 1991.

The year 1883 was also eventful for the black community because the First Baptist Church started construction in the same year as its new school. The First Baptist Church was located on Meadow Street in a frame building similar to that of the Episcopal church. Worship services were held in the basement until the completion of the sanctuary.[139] Many of the materials and much of the labor was provided by individual members of the church. Dr. David N. Vassar was pastor. In 1967, the First Baptist Church was provided with a brick veneer. The first public school for black students was built in 1883 in the Louisa Courthouse District on West Street. The frame building consisted of two rooms.[140] This served for black education until 1926.

Chapter 14

Louisa in the News

On October 3, 1884, the *News and Farmer* reported:

> *About two years ago a test case was begun to try the legality of the Louisa Restrictions. Our readers understand fully the nature of the restrictions. At the recent term of the circuit court, Judge Barton decided in favor of Mr. Trice, the present owner, of the Hotel, holding that the deed conveying these restrictions was ol* [sic] *in law and the purchaser of them ran no risk of having them removed, no matter how he used his property—declaring that a man had a right to use his property as he pleased.*

Mr. Trice and the hotel were once again in the news.

On a cold night on January 8, 1888, catastrophe hit the town. On this night, the town of Louisa was struck by fire. With the town busy recovering from the fire, the Fredericksburg and Richmond newspapers are our only sources of contemporary news about the fire.

In the *Richmond Times Dispatch*, the headline was:

LOUISA'S BIG BLAZE
NEARLY THE WHOLE BUSINESS PART OF THE TOWN IN ASHES

> *Last night about 10:30 o'clock a fire originated in the store of Lazarus Bib (colored)—flames—broke out in the building. Nearly the entire business portion of the town was in a mass of ruins by 2 A.M.*
>
> *The buildings which burned were on the North side of Main Street in downtown Louisa. The fire that struck the town of Louisa caused other communities to consider the safety of their own towns. In Bowling Green, it was suggested that their town supply themselves with water, since their businesses were of wood, mostly, and adjoining each other. Nearly half the buildings in Louisa were insured. The damage was severe for those who did not have insurance. It was reported that R. P. Cammack, H. M. Daniel, Leon Levy, Jr., William Ira Kennon, Pendleton and Son, W. M. Young, Virgil Perkins, J. B. Levy and Andrew Shelton*

> *had insurance. J. K. Pettus, Mr. Schuman, C. N. Hester, J. M. and J. F. Bickers, W. E. Bibb and George Shelton had no insurance.*
>
> *Notwithstanding the bright morning, Main Street presents a forlorn appearance. The goods were all conveyed across to the courthouse side and parties interested are busily engaged assorting and conveying them to places of safety. The mud is ankle deep, and the goods would scarcely be recognized as the article of yesterday morning.*
>
> *At this hour, it is hard to learn the exact status of affairs. Everybody worked manfully, but in the absence of fire-apparatus and water the only thing to be done was to remove goods and valuables as quickly as possible. Fortunately nobody was killed or seriously hurt.*[141]

The *Louisa Weekly Record* wrote on May 13, 1876 (twelve years prior to the 1888 fire), that "buckets, ladders etc. are kept in the cellar of Dr. Beadles' store." The fire alarm was the courthouse bell, which was supposed to be rung for fifteen minutes if there was a fire. In 1888, the drawback was obvious—if the equipment was in a burning building, it was useless. This might have been the case during the 1888 fire.

Some businesses rebuilt immediately. The 1889 land tax lists new buildings erected by R.P. Cammack, Mitch Mills, William Ira Kennon and Virgil Perkins. These stores were mostly built of brick. William Ira Kennon was the life and fire insurance salesman in Louisa. It was likely that business improved for him after the fire.

Evidently, the fire in Louisa interrupted the operations of the town council, which did not meet again until June 9, 1888, at Dr. Pendleton's Drug Store. At that meeting, the council reviewed the building of a town hall, and business as usual began again.

The new hotel narrowly survived the 1888 fire. The building was erected by Rice P. Cammack in 1887. "R.P. Cammack tore down the old tavern and erected a very handsome and commodious new hotel on the same site at a cost of about $9000.00."[142] The hotel was integral to the history of the village. From the 1890s through the 1920s, Louisa was known as a summer resort. The Louisa Hotel and several private homes took in boarders during the summer months. People living in Richmond and the Peninsula would travel to Louisa to get away from the hot and humid cities and for relaxed country living.

An attack on the hotel was begun in 1893 under the flag of the temperance movement. The town council received the following on April 10, 1893:

> *To the Town Council of Louisa*
> *Gentlemen*
> *As I am Christianly opposed to licensing the sale of intoxicating liquors and believe that the license law is a sin against God and a crime against man, I sign this petition with a feeling of humiliation that we live in a state that has so infamous a law on the statute books. As your honorable body has not the authority to grant or withhold license, but simply to fix the amount. My name is appended, asking that that amount be high.*
>
> *Respectfully yours, L.A. Cutler*[143]

Landon A. Cutler was the minister of the Louisa Christian Church for twenty-one years. Twenty-one other gentlemen joined him in his petition for higher taxes on the sale of liquor. One of the signers, A.D. Arnett, had tested the restrictions on the sale of spirits in town just three years earlier in order to sell liquor himself. There must have been a rapid conversion on his part. Three days later, a petition signed by forty-eight prominent ladies of the town was also presented to the council. "We ask the tax be raised to $500." Landon Cutler was to run for governor of Virginia in the 1897 election as a nominee for the Prohibition Party.

In the 1890s, William E. Bibb, a former state senator and Louisa resident, organized the effort to contest the road laws of the time. Courthouse records for the first part of the century were mostly concerned with the roads, which were in disreputable condition. The roads were often so bad that only the horses were able to slug through the mud and the mire. The roads were maintained by the same private workforces that had been maintaining the roads since the 1700s. The labor tax required that all able-bodied men between the ages of sixteen and sixty work on the county roads for two days each year. If they refused, they were fined a one-dollar tax. "Pete" Proffitt refused to work or pay the fine and he was arrested. After a failed appeal, he applied to the Virginia Supreme Court of Appeals for a writ of habeas corpus for false imprisonment. William Bibb, son-in-law of John C. Cammack, took the case to contest the road laws. On February 1, 1894, the court decision declared the road tax unconstitutional by Virginia law. This judgment placed the responsibility for the building and maintenance of roads on the county, with no assistance from state or federal government. One long-term result of this case was the creation of a State Highway Commission in 1906.[144]

Louisa was the only large town in Louisa County until Mineral City Mining, Manufacturing and Land Company was incorporated in 1890. Mineral was a planned town, created to meet the demands of new residents who worked in the local mines. The first officers of the land company were, in the majority, residents of the town of Louisa. R.P. Talley was president with fellow officers W.R. Goodwin and P.B. Porter. Directors included W.E. Bibb, W.O. Smith, J.F. Bickers and J.W. Flanagan. All of these men lived in the town of Louisa and joined with outside interests to form the town of Mineral. As the years went by, Louisa felt the competition of having another town in the county. It was suggested on several occasions that the courthouse should be moved to Mineral because Mineral was closer to the center of the county.

Mineral, as the only other town in the county, developed its own newspapers in the early 1900s. Mineral published the *Mineral Mirror* in 1904. M.B. Quisenberry was president and Dr. James Garland Boxley Sr. was editor. In 1907, this paper merged with the *Louisa Enterprise*. Mineral later established the *Mineral Weekly Progress*, which ran from 1916 to 1917.[145]

Chapter 15

Turn of the Century in Louisa

New buildings were being erected in the town of Louisa at and around the turn of the century. Dr. Harry W. Porter and his wife Josephine Norris Porter bought land in 1901 and built a home adjacent to what would become the fireman's field. It is a fine example of the Queen Ann style of Victorian-era architecture with its typical gable detailing. The building was subsequently bought by the Woodwards and converted to a funeral home in 1937.

The freight station was built in 1892 and the passenger station in 1902 by the Chesapeake and Ohio Rail Road Company. The passenger station is of board-and-batten construction, in the Gothic style. These were boom years for the railroad.

The first telephones in the county were installed by Judge F.W. Sims. The phones were connected by a private line that ran between his home in the town of Louisa and his farm in Apple Grove. The Louisa Telephone Company, formed as the result of a charter application filed in June of 1898, began a new era of communication in Louisa County. James O. Winston was the first president, S. Crenshaw of Richmond was vice-president, T.S. Winston was secretary/treasurer and J.J. Mills and F.W. Sims were directors. The first proposed phone lines were to extend from the Louisa Courthouse to Apple Grove via Mineral City, Pendleton Station or Cuckoo; from Louisa Courthouse to Poindexter's Store via Trevilians and Lasley; from Poindexter's Store to Zion to Gordonsville; from Louisa Courthouse to Bells X Roads to Yanceyville; from Louisa Courthouse to Ellisville and Bibb Store Road; and from Thompson's X Roads to Shelton Mill.[146]

After the company was chartered in 1898, Mrs. Ada Flannagan, an early switchboard operator who worked with the telephone company for twenty-five years, listed the first phone subscribers. The list for Louisa included the Bank of Louisa, F.M. Beale, W.E. Bibb, J.J. Boxley, Floyd Chaney, C&O Railway Depot, the county clerk's office, W.J. Crank, B.L. Dickinson, H.Q. Dickinson, C.W. Donnally, W.R. Dunkum, A.F. Estes, Mrs. S.H. Flannagan, H.H. Hiter, J.A. Kent, Kent's Drug Store, the Louisa Drug Store, the Louisa Hotel, J.W. Nunn, Jesse Porter, Mrs. Wilmer Sims, Dr. W.O. Smith, Mrs. W.R. Goodwin and A.B. Woodward. For Mineral, D.E. Bumpass was the only name on the list. For Trevilians, the list included the Trevilian Depot and Lee Rosson. H.H.

Louisa Depot. *Courtesy of Mrs. Aubrey Seay.*

Walton Lumber Company at Pendleton was also listed.[147] By 1903, the Western Union Telegraph Company, Louisa Telephone Company and Adams Express Company were licensed and taxed by the town council.[148]

The J. Lewis Dobbins building at one time served as a post office and contained the telephone exchange. The lot upon which the Dobbins building now stands was once a part of the "Old Dragon" lot and was later a part of the Nannie W. Vaughan estate. It is not known why the lot was called the Old Dragon, but it sounds like a tavern name.

Restrictions on personal property in the town of Louisa ended in 1904. Restrictions on the sale of spirits had been placed on all land sold in the town of Louisa since 1816. By allowing only the hotel owner to sell liquor, the restrictions essentially created a monopoly. This product was a profitable enterprise for the hotel owner because of the courthouse activities. In 1890, A.D. Arnett creatively tested the limits of the alcohol restrictions by trying to prove that his land was on county property within courthouse boundaries, in which case he would be free to sell spirits. He lost. In 1904, H.Q. Dickinson and his wife Mary Hawse owned the hotel and lived at what is today the Whistle Stop Bed and Breakfast. They accepted $1,500 cash from about thirty-four property owners in the town of Louisa to end the alcohol restrictions on individual properties and the monopoly ended.[149] The temperance movement undoubtedly affected their choice. Louisa was a popular tourist site in the summer. Several years prior to 1904, the voters of the district voted "no license" to sell whiskey—the hotel lost its bar and bar rights and the district was dry.[150] The property restrictions of 1816 also excluded the operation of eateries and taverns from property owners in the town, so the Dickinsons did give up

Mayor Johnson was a descendant of Thomas Johnson. *Courtesy of Marjorie Lee Woolfolk.*

sole proprietorship of tourist sites. Though the town was no longer under a one-man monopoly, the owners of the hotel continued to be important to town politics.

On July 7, 1909, the town council passed ordinances against the sale of cider by street vendors within the town limits.[151] The restricted cider had at least a 6 percent content of alcohol and was called "near beer." These ordinances were passed, rescinded and reinstated in the same year. Still, the sale of liquor was permitted at the hotel. In a small town like Louisa, these ordinances were often passed because of a local incident involving drunkenness. James Craig of Rose Cliff Fruit Farms Inc. questioned the restrictions when his vendor R.E. Scruggs was fined for selling two glasses of cider to William Belvin in July of the same year. Mr. Craig felt that the Town of Louisa prevented him from carrying out his lawful business and caused him great damage by the continued enforcement of the ordinances. Mr. Craig sued Mayor George H. Johnson and the town council. In September, the defendant Mr. Scruggs was found guilty and fined twenty-five dollars. Mr. Craig appealed to the Virginia Supreme Court of Appeals in September of 1909 and was refused a writ of error.[152] The courts upheld the rights of the board of trustees to pass ordinances. In the suit, it was brought out that though the town only had three hundred inhabitants, at least four hundred people lived in the area in proximity to the courthouse. The majority of the people in Louisa were religious and felt that the sale and misuse of spirits should be carefully monitored. According to the town minutes, street vendors selling cider were considered a nuisance unless regulated. The first resolution stated, "No person shall sell cider of any kind, or 'near beer' in the Town of Louisa and within one mile except in some building as a place of business but not any building used for any other business."[153]

Changes in the town continued with the building of a new courthouse in 1905. Complaints about the poor condition of the courthouse started in 1896. Finally, in 1904, the decision was made to build a new courthouse. The *Supervisors Journal* contains a petition from the new Town of Mineral on June 18, 1904: "On a petition from the Citizens of Mineral to erect the new Court House at their town and making an offer of $5000 for its erection." The board was unanimously opposed to moving the courthouse away from Louisa. It asked for contributions from the people of Louisa to offset the offer from Mineral. The discussion to move the courthouse to Mineral did not end there. The next month, the records stated that the commonwealth's attorney advised that the courthouse could not be moved without further legislation. The board was resolved that it did not have the power to move the courthouse away from the town of Louisa. The motion to proceed to build the new courthouse on county property was deadlocked and a tiebreaker was called for, resulting in the building of the fourth courthouse.[154]

The courthouse that was built in 1905 is the current Louisa County Courthouse and it is the architectural centerpiece of the town of Louisa. The 1905 courthouse replaced the prior 1818 courthouse and the clerks office after both buildings were condemned as unsafe in April of 1896.[155] The base of the 1905 courthouse was built with brick taken from the wall that surrounded the 1818 courthouse. A debate by board members ended in a decision to keep the law office and to tear down the clerk's office. The older building, the 1830s law office, still stands on the courthouse lawn. The courthouse built in the Colonial Revival style was designed by Wiley D. Anderson and C.K. Howells,

Street vendors on Main Street, Louisa. *Courtesy of Ann Avery Hunter.*

The town pump can be seen in front of the 1905 courthouse. *Courtesy of the Griswold Boxley Collection.*

architects from Richmond, Virginia. The contractors for the work were George Leigh & Brothers of Louisa. The courthouse is a temple-form public building with classical details. Two relics of the older courthouse were retained. The old bell still hangs at the courthouse and the stone steps sit on the courthouse lawn.

The ladies of Louisa formed the Louisa Confederate Monument Association in the spring of 1902 to erect a monument dedicated to local Confederate soldiers on the courthouse lawn. This monument was finished in combination with the new courthouse. William L. Shepherd, an artist from Richmond, designed the monument, and Mr. William Sievers, from New York, was the sculptor. The monument arrived from New York and Richmond via the C&O railroad and was erected by Mr. A.J. Wray.[156]

The Louisa County Courthouse and the Confederate monument were both dedicated on August 17, 1905, with a huge crowd in attendance. Veterans of the War Between the States held a reunion at the same event. The event was compared to "March Court Day" in a speech by the historian Porter Wright: "People would come to Louisa in March to see who had lived through the winter and in December to get their Christmas 'likker.' They also brought every conceivable object which they thought they could sell or swap. It has been estimated that literally thousands of persons would gather here on those days some travelling all night to arrive here for the big day." A comment on the size of the crowd was made by the late John Bibb, who had attended a presidential inauguration in Washington. Someone there remarked on the size of the crowd and John, drawing himself up in all of his dignity, laid him low by saying: "Hell, man, you have never seen a crowd until you have been to Louisa Courthouse on a March Court Day."[157] The March Court Day described by Bibb occurred prior to the invention of the automobile. Later court days would attract smaller crowds. In the early 1900s, March Court Day was generally a man's day. The ladies would stay indoors, visiting friends around the town. The meeting day in August, during the same era, was termed a "Trades Day" or "Watermelon Court."[158]

The village lawn was the location of much activity for the town of Louisa. In early days, it held the stocks and pillories. In 1902, it was reported that the last man was executed by hanging in Louisa on the courthouse green. He was hanged on the gallows in front of the jail. Politicians used the front steps of the courthouse for speeches and people congregated there to read notices on the courthouse wall. Even circuses and festivals have been held on the lawn.

As a result of their proximity, the town and county often needed to work together. In May of 1906, the chairman of the board of supervisors requested that the town accept half of the cost of erecting horse racks around the courthouse and jail.[159] The

Robert Barret on the courthouse lawn with his daughters and their young friends. *Courtesy of Dickie Leake.*

horse racks comprised a simple construction of poles for tying the reins of horses and carriages. Improvements such as this were not considered useful with the advent of the automobile.

A major improvement in 1906 was the addition of granolithic walks in the town. A bond issue was passed for the public sidewalks and they were finished by December of 1906.[160] These walks replaced the previous sidewalks that consisted of tan bark. Efforts were also made to bring water and electric lights to town.

A report in September of 1906 asked the town to list private and public improvements that had been completed in town, such as the construction of a city hall, the fire engine house and the installation of electric lights, water works, sewers and pavements.[161] According to the town minutes, sidewalks were laid by December. A well and water system existed, but the systems were continually improved. A new system was installed in 1909. Electric lights were not available in the town. The council was asked for underground acetylene gas pipes to be laid in 1911. Acetylene gas pipes could have provided a bright-burning gas to street lamps. Whether they were actually laid is unknown. Calling into question the availability of an alternate power was the fact that W.H. Vaden was still tending the oil lanterns on posts in 1916. The town minutes didn't mention any sort of power company until 1925. The franchise for lighting the town was awarded to the Louisa County Light and Power Company in July of 1925 and a plant was erected in Mineral. The power company was to light all streetlights, businesses and residences in the town of Louisa within five months. "The Louisa Light and Power Company which began operation March 1, 1926 has set out to provide electric light and power service to the whole of the county and to provide agricultural sections with a utility which they have not enjoyed before."[162] It was over ten years before the Rural Electrification Association brought electricity to the county in 1936.

On July 6, 1906, the town council supported giving $150 to supplement the salary of a high school teacher, should such a teacher be appointed, and $50 for the repair of the school building and the grading of ground for Haley High.[163] The building of a new high school was also in the works. The first planned housing development was established during the early years of 1900, and the new high school was the centerpiece. Mary Gooch planned lots surrounding the new school in 1906, but only a few houses were built. The first building on the sold property was not worth less than $1,500. The Sargeant and Hart homes were built later on both sides of the school, but the planned streets were never realized.

The Louisa High School property was located about two blocks from the Louisa County Courthouse square. Close to three acres of land was bought, to be used as school grounds, in April of 1907 by the Louisa Courthouse District School Board. The building of the school was the result of two actions—the new Virginia State Constitution of 1902 made possible educational reforms, and the Mann High School bill appropriated $50,000 to communities that would provide the buildings and match state funds. Louisa was the first county to take advantage of the state-matching funds designated for free public education.[164]

A one-and-a-half-story structure designed by Charles M. Robinson was built by the Leigh brothers. The building was constructed of stone that had been quarried from land known as the Bernard Daniel place on Fredericksburg Avenue. Called the Louisa High School, the building housed students from grades one through eleven. Later, a smaller building was erected for overflow students.

The town council was advised of a problem with the train and the school in 1907. The train evidently stopped for longer than twenty minutes (which was unlawful) and held up students and teachers who were on their way home. Some of the children aggravated matters by climbing under the train, which scared the teachers present. The teachers asked that the town council complain to the train company.[165]

By 1911, the new high school included a normal training department that provided a year of teacher training. Between 1910 and 1921, a second story and an auditorium were added to the new high school. In 1924, a fire swept through the building, leaving only the shell. Fortunately, the auditorium was not damaged by the fire. The building was rebuilt by Elgin Morris and was reopened in 1925.

A 1909 suit stated that "the town had a first grade Normal and High School and a colored graded School with a large number of pupils from the surrounding county."[166]

Miss Lucile Holt, a native of Louisa County, was appointed to serve as the first Jeanes Supervisor for the Louisa County Negro Schools.[167] Under her supervision, the quality of instruction improved, the length of the school term expanded and salaries for teachers increased. In 1921, the Rosenwald Foundation Building was erected in the Louisa District for the black community. Secondary school subjects were offered there and five students attended high school in the same building. The Louisa Training School for blacks was built by Julius Rosenwald in the late 1920s. This was a five-room consolidated school located adjacent to the present-day Thomasson's Funeral Home in the town of Louisa. Grades one through eleven were taught there. Carl Perkins recalls, "I started to this school as a first grader in 1927 and graduated in 1938. This school had no inside plumbing, central heat, library, gym, or cafeteria. At the beginning of the school day, the first thing students had to do was to start the fire in the pot-bellied stove. The last thing in the evening was to get the wood in for the day."[168] Mrs. Zelda C. Morton was supervisor and Reverend B.B. Ellis the first principal. It became the first high school for African Americans to be accredited by the Virginia State Board of Education. This school served the community until 1953. The A.G. Richardson High School was opened to replace the training school east of the town of Louisa.

In April of 1911, the town and county joined funds to build a water tower. The county paid two-thirds and the town one-third of the total bill. The county wanted a fire hydrant located near the courthouse and jail. Using the water tower and the deep well sunk in 1908, some water and sewer pipes were laid. S.S. Griffith was allowed to run a pipe, at his own expense, to the hotel from the deep well owned by the town and county jointly. The town charged $1.50 for the first spigot and $1.00 for each additional spigot.[169] Later an agreement was reached between the county and town whereby the county relinquished its entire interest in the well and the pump to the town on the condition that the town supplied the courthouse, jail and

Louisa Training School. In 1954, John Thomasson bought his former high school in order to open up a funeral home. *Courtesy of the* Central Virginian.

public hydrant for the sum of $12.50 per month. Eleven years later, the board of supervisors ordered the town council to remove the water tank in the courthouse "owing to the insecurity of present water tank in the courthouse building and the danger of damage to said building on account of water leaking through the jury room and then into the Clerks Office."[170]

One reason the Presbyterian church was built at the end of Depot Street may have been that the planned neighborhood was never actually developed. The church was erected in 1911, after the membership separated from Wills Memorial Chapel in the Green Springs area. The new church was started by thirteen members who lived in the town or nearby. The land for the church was donated by Mr. Charles W. Donnally; the Reverend Hugh H. Hudson, the minister of Wills Memorial Chapel, organized and helped to build the church. In 1919, the church purchased a manse across the street. An addition to the church was completed by August of 1949. There was a Methodist church at one end of Depot Street and the Presbyterians at the other end—the street was later renamed Church Avenue.

The new buildings were reported in the local newspaper, the *Central Virginian*, which was established by L.S. Pendleton in 1912. F.G. Duvall was the secretary/treasurer and L.R. Driver the manager of the paper.[171] The *Central Virginian* is still the only newspaper for Louisa County.

A bigger development was being built in Westover in 1914 on the opposite side of town. George V. Venable and Kiah T. Ford bought twenty-nine acres from Kate C. Bibb, the widow of W.E. Bibb. The land was divided into streets and lots with craftsman-style houses. This area remains much the same as it was when first built.

When the town was incorporated, town safety was considered in the ordinance that stated "no person should be permitted to strain a horse or drive a vehicle at dangerous speed." Cars had become a part of Louisa life by 1914, and the town found it necessary to enact a resolution in 1914 that the speed limit for automobiles in the town of Louisa should not exceed eight miles per hour.[172]

Mrs. Manning Woodward Sr. described her first experience with a car in Louisa. Mrs. Woodward and her sister, both young girls, were on their way to town for a music lesson in a horse-drawn buggy. "Dr. Woolfolk approached us in his car. Our horse became frightened and took out across the field, with sheet music and lap robes flying all over the place. Dr. Woolfolk stopped his car and caught the horse and got us settled on our way again."[173] J.A. Kent was permitted to erect a gasoline tank and pump in front of the Kent Drug Store on Main Street in 1915.[174] Woodward Motors began operations in 1918, selling Chevrolets and Oldsmobiles, and continued in the car business for at least thirty-one years.[175] Another early car dealer was J. Frank Sargeant, who expanded his Louisa Hardware Company to include car sales and a garage. However, in 1915, a resolution that all privies in town be made fly-proof indicates that technology was lacking in some areas.[176]

Citizens who feared the dangerous speeds of the new motorcars sent this petition to the mayor in 1919:

> *To Dr. H. S. Daniel, Mayor of the town of Louisa and town council*
> *We the citizens & business people of the Town of Louisa realizing the danger to little children and old people when crossing Main Street from the fast cars and trucks, we earnestly beg Dr. H. S. Daniel Mayor of the Town of Louisa and the Town Council to pass a town ordinance making the speed limit through the corporate limits not to exceed 15 miles per hour and have such laws be enacted, rigidly enforced regardless of who the guilty one may be, so that our little ones may have some protection while crossing the street.*[177]

The town council passed the following ordinance in 1918, a reaction to wartime conditions: "Whereas, it is the duty of all patriotic citizens to discourage loafing in the time of war."[178] The ordinance provides little insight into the state of affairs during the war. The town encouraged local men to join the service for their country. One of the men who answered the call, Joseph L. Wills, would eventually become the town mayor. Another was William Earle Crank, who answered a questionnaire from the War History Commission for the State of Virginia after the war.[179] Mr. Crank was born in 1891 and joined the infantry as a private in November of 1917. He was in Company C, 136th M.G. Battalion of the 37th Division. He arrived in Brest in July of 1917. He participated in Baccarat Sector, Avacouth Sector and Meuse-Argonne Offensives as a corporal, during which participation he was slightly wounded. One soldier who enlisted at the courthouse was James L. Gilliam.

Women from the town of Louisa also served in the First World War. Evelyn Maude Johnson was born on June 11, 1884, in the town of Louisa. Her father was George H. Johnson, mayor from 1915 to 1925, and her mother was Laura Buck. After joining the service, Evelyn was sent to Norfolk on September 11, 1918, where she did clerical work as a stenographer. She was discharged from the naval base at Hampton Roads, Virginia. Her father ran the Louisa Hotel for many years, served as mayor and was a descendant of Thomas Johnson.

In 1920, the United States passed Prohibition laws that lasted until 1933. Mayor George McDuffie Blake lived next to St. James Episcopal Church and was a congregant there. Since the church kept its doors unlocked, Blake's wife Emma kept the communion wine at their home in a closet to keep it safe from thieves during Prohibition.[180]

In 1921, the State Highway Department built a hard-surfaced road through the town of Louisa. Prior to 1921, West Street served as the road to Gordonsville. The new road ran along the side of the railroad to avoid crossing the tracks twice in the town. At one time previously, the road (the Spotswood Trail) crossed the railroad tracks twelve times as it ran through Louisa County. The town for some years maintained the streets within the town limits, but by 1930, the town allowed the Highway Commission to take over what was then called Route 39. The number changed to Route 33 and again to Route 22 over the years and is now called the Jefferson Davis Highway.

The county was constantly changing the use of the courthouse offices. In 1922, the board of supervisors did not rerent an office in the courthouse that had been occupied by local lawyers Gordon, Gordon and Crank. The sheriff and deputy sheriff had applied for use of the office. There were no rules to decide the use of county property. When the county no longer provided office space to individuals, the lawyers had to rent offices in the town. There were several small buildings in town that were used as law offices for individual lawyers. The use of county property for private business harkens back to days of Thomas Johnson and his use of the jail for storing grain. His example was apparently imitated through the years.

Town Mayor George McDuffie Blake owned the paper the *Central Virginian* from 1924 to 1940. The paper was then bought by Bruce V. Boxley, who owned the paper from 1940 until his death in 1955.

According to Mr. Henry Woolfolk's notes, the fire department was first organized in the spring of 1924, with Mr. R.M. Flanagan as chief. However, the minutes of the town council mention a fire hydrant in 1911 as an adjunct to a new water tower. And later in 1923, a firehouse is mentioned as being near an artesian well.[181] Considering the drastic fire in the town of Louisa in 1888, official development of a fire department was very slow. In 1926, a meeting of the town council called for the organization of a fire company. This happened because Mr. E.S. Hensen, a native of Denmark, resigned as fire chief.

Mayor George McDuffie Blake. *Courtesy of the Griswold Boxley Collection.*

Firemen stand in front of the Bank of Louisa. Otis Rupert Thompson sits on the front of the fire engine, Henry Bascomb Hunter stands next to the wheel, Henry Woolfolk stands behind him in the white coat and Richard E. Perkins is in front of the back wheel. *Courtesy of Ann Avery Hunter.*

On February 19, 1929, fire officers gained approval to create a fire company and to render assistance at fires. This date is recognized as the official start of the Louisa Fire Company and of much-needed assistance to a large area of the county. In 1931, a new fire hall was built.

The fireman's fair in the town of Louisa was begun as a result of the purchase of a 1935 Seagraves, a fire truck that could pump five hundred gallons per minute. The first fair was held to help pay for the truck, which was under threat of repossession.[182] It was a one-day fair on the Fourth of July. Mayor George McDuffie Blake invited President Franklin Delano Roosevelt to the Louisa Fair and the president responded that he would give the invitation due consideration.[183] Roosevelt's motorcade did drive through Louisa on fair day, his second visit to Louisa. Mayor Blake was a Roosevelt man and felt he deserved recognition for that. His feelings were stated in an editorial in the *Central Virginian* in December of 1932: "I state this because of the fact that in July 1931, upon my invitation as Mayor of the Town of Louisa, Governor Roosevelt stopped over in our town, accompanied by our distinguished Governor John Garland Pollard, and I assured Mr. Roosevelt that he would not only get the nomination but would be elected. I had a hunch so I'm regarded in our town as the original Roosevelt man." In 1932, the fair was held on the land of Henry Woolfolk, the fire chief. The Louisa Medical Center is now located on that land.[184] The fireman's fair is still an annual event in the town of Louisa.

Besides the fireman's fair, small circuses often came to town, with sometimes-explosive results. A big elephant fight near Louisa Courthouse occurred in May of 1887. There were eight elephants involved. "Emperor, a bull that had been around the show for many years; Chief, Princess, and Mary and four unaccountable others—Radjak, Caliph, Woodah, and Bismark, the latter and Princess being for the African species."[185] Chief was credited with starting the melee by attacking Bismark, but before it was over, the rest of the eight took sides.[186] These elephants probably belonged to the John Robinson Circus.

Car dealerships were well established by 1926. "Woodard-Vaughan Motor Co. established in Louisa January 1, 1925 to deal in Buick and Chevrolet automobiles, has now reached proportions which place it among the largest automobile agencies in this section. Mr. Woodward has been in automotive business since 1919."[187] Joining Mr. Woodward in the 1930s were Jesse Hadder's Ford Company and W.A.C. Pettit's Chrysler dealership.

The *Central Virginian* remarked upon the progress of the town of Louisa in 1926. Thomas Lafayette Woolfolk was appointed postmaster in 1922. Mr. Woolfolk's family was also mentioned in the paper. His son was a member of Perkins and Woolfolk, one of the county's largest stores. His two daughters worked with him in the post office. The post office was soon to be rated a second-class facility, indicating substantial growth. The government of Louisa was a big factor in the growth and development of the town and was noted to have "given the town good lighting, system of general utilities which will rank among the best in any community of similar size in the State of Virginia."[188]

There is no mention of the Great Depression in the minutes of the town council. The event went unremarked. The local newspaper did follow the Depression as it progressed

J. Frank Sergeant Hardware Store, which later expanded to form a Ford dealership. *Courtesy of the* Central Virginian.

nationally but made little comment about its effects on the town. Banking ads were front-page items and included sayings such as, "Worry is a disease for which money in the bank is the best medicine."[189] Both the National Bank and the Bank of Louisa were still operating after the Depression. Likewise, many of the lead businesses survived the Depression and, in fact, many of the family names advertised in 1929 are still present in today's business news. J.S. Purcell was vice-president of the Bank of Louisa and T.S. Winston held said office at the First National Bank. A.C. Marshall was distributor for the Virginia Feed and Seed, W.A. Ellis managed the Louisa Service Station, Woodward and Vaughan Motors sold Chevrolets and R.B. Massie and J. Frank Sargeant ran hardware stores. J. Quintus Massie spoke of the Depression's effects on Louisa farmers: "Then came the stock market collapse in 1929, and the banks closing in 1932. We were not affected so much by the stock market, that was for rich people, but the bank closing affected everyone. Prices for corn, wheat, tobacco and cattle all dropped very low."[190]

Despite hard times, life continued. Hattie Crebbs was hired to work for the Ford Motor Company after graduating from high school in 1934. Mr. Jesse Hadder ran the Ford dealership, located on Main Street, where Ed Whitlock's boat and motor company is located today in Louisa. One day, Hattie drove to the drugstore in town and parked in front; when she left the store, she hopped in the car and drove back to work. It seems Mr. Joe Porter's car looked just like hers. When he left his store in the evening, his car was gone, locked up in the Hadder garage. Evidently, everyone left their keys in their cars at that time.[191]

The town council was shocked by the death of its mayor, Joseph L. Wills, in January of 1930. A war veteran, Mayor Wills was instrumental in the establishment of the town water system. The following year, the first women were elected to the town council. On September 4, 1931, Lucy Goodwin Donnally (Mrs. J.P.) and Rosa Woodward joined the formerly all-male town council. No reaction from the former male bastion could be found in the town council minutes or in the newspaper, even though the ladies did oust one incumbent councilman. The councilmen had to take a no-dueling oath. The first record found of this oath was in 1929: "I swear that I have not, while a citizen of this state, since the twentieth day of July, Nineteen hundred and two, fought a duel with a deadly weapon."[192] It is doubtful that ladies were considered when this oath was created. The ladies signed this oath the day after their election.

In 1932, the Byrd Road Law "lifted Virginia out of the Mud."[193] The law relieved the counties from the duty of maintaining roads. Main Street was paved with concrete about 1926, but the rural roads were still in terrible condition. In 1932, a map from the Department of Highways shows two hard-surfaced roads in Louisa County, Route 15 and Route 33. Most of Route 522 and some of Route 250 are marked as soil, gravel, sand and clay roads. Most of the county roads were unimproved or graded but not surfaced. John Q. Rhodes of Louisa created the Porter-Rhodes Act with Daniel L. Porter of Orange in 1930 to ensure that the state paved 1,587 miles of farm-to-market roads in the state. Mr. Rhodes went on to become director of the Division of Motor Vehicles under Governor Peery, where he campaigned for highway safety. Mr. Rhodes built a house across from the new Louisa High School called Rhodes Folly. His home was on land that was called the old race field.

Boy Scouts were a part of the school system in 1938. *Front, seated*: Junior Jones, James Swartz. *Second row, left to right*: Henry Vaughan, Carrol Clark, Gale Wray, Allen Flannagan, Russell McDonall, Charles Ransone, William Frazier. *Standing, left to right*: Clifton Vawter, Donald Lee Atkins, Linden Chiles, Lindsay Gordon, Pet Morris, John Sam Purcell, Albert Hensen, Harry "Beany" Hallet and Robert Chiles. Not pictured are Alfred Biggerstaff, Bobby Boyd, James McCarrick and John Gilmer. *Courtesy of Christine Southard.*

In 1937, a fire tower was built about a mile west of the courthouse in Louisa. It is now in the town limits but was not at the time it was built. The 102-foot-tall Louisa Fire Tower was used to detect fires and to monitor enemy aircraft during World War II. It was built by the Civil Conservation Corps on land purchased from the Bibb family. Ten counties can be viewed from the tower, including Fluvanna and Orange. Women outnumbered men as operators (or lookouts) at the tower in the spring fire season. Howard Scheurenbrand, Louisa County forester, claimed that most men couldn't deal with the height.[194] In 1995, the Louisa Fire Tower was inducted into the National Historic Lookout Register. It was the third so designated in the state.

In 1937, Sheriff J.F. Bickers took the Town of Louisa and the board of supervisors to task for renting one of his rooms in the jail. The board, on May 8, 1937, rented one room to the Town of Louisa. In the past, rooms had been rented out for business concerns, but this room was rented to the Louisa town sergeant to hold prisoners. Sheriff Bickers felt the board did not have the power to rent the room without the approval of a judge. He wanted to keep the room available for female prisoners. In this case, compromise was the outcome. The board was allowed to rent out the room, but the sheriff was in charge of how and when it was used.[195] This dispute is an indication of the growing

Girl Scouts in 1938. *Back row, left to right*: Helen Poore, Eleanor Chiles (Thompson), Frances Ann Henson (Atkins), Marjorie Timberlake, Frances Timberlake, Dorothea "Dot" Lynch, Martha Jean Woodward, Ann Nichols, Betty Morris (Vaughan), Elaine Bray, Elizabeth "Sis" Perkins, Flora Biggerstaff. *Front row, left to right*: Frances Cunningham (McGehee), Linda Crank, Mary Ann Loving (Mins), Rosa Lee Chapman, Blair Hunt (Sharp), Bobbie Gallion, Virginia McDonald (Guisto), Dorothy "Dot" Grey Rosson, Iris Southard (Pleasants), Arlene Shumake, Blanche Perkins and Gwendolyn Cain. Marianne Ransone is not pictured. *Courtesy of Christine Southard.*

pains of the town and the sometimes-contentious interaction of the town and county. It seems that the use of the jail was a bone of contention for a few more years, as well. In the town minutes of 1943, a controversy over the closing of the jail is indicated, but no more information is available. County Sheriff Ashland Fortune was town sergeant in 1964. He remembers that the town paid ten dollars a day for the county jail to hold town prisoners at that time. The 1868 jail was used by the county until 1968, when it was condemned as one of the four worst jails in Virginia.

In 1940, the three high schools in the county consolidated with a new school built outside of Mineral. The old Louisa High School became an elementary facility and it was used in that capacity for forty-four years. In 1984, the elementary school was replaced with a new central facility a few miles east of Louisa and the older school closed. W.A.C. Pettit III, who lived next door in the Sargeant house, purchased the land and the school building.

Two other old school buildings are still standing in the town. The original 1877 high school is a private home on Elm Street. John Thomasson bought his former high school, the Louisa Training School, and erected a funeral home on the property in front of the school.

In 1941, the Town of Louisa considered using the town management system for the running of the town. Until this time, and for many years afterward, only secretaries served the town. The idea of employing the town management system in Louisa was defeated in the May election.

Chapter 16

World War II and the Growth of the Town and County

War once again took young men from the town and county of Louisa upon the advent of World War II. Mrs. Netty Trainum remarked on the times:

On the home front minute men were organized from the old, young and disabled who were not able to go to war. Their job was to patrol the streets and march on Sundays. They had uniforms with metal hats issued by the government.[196] *Volunteer airplane spotters were placed county wide. Each house had dark green shades which "blacked out" the interior lights so that homes could not be seen in the night. Many citizens of Louisa relied upon their feet to get from place to place. Even bikes could not be used because troop convoys were often so long that the roads could not be used. The young people were able to participate in the war effort by buying 10 cent stamps which could be used to fill up a U.S. Saving Bond.*[197]

Mrs. Anna Seay also commented on the era:

For women and rural inhabitants of Louisa, meat, milk and eggs were no problem but the lack of tires and gas was a hardship. One way for women to serve was as a cadet nurse. Participation in the cadet nurse classes prepared women to become army and navy nurses with commissions. In 1945 the last cadet class was predominantly made up of women. In the 1940s there was still no electricity in some of the rural areas. The women, studying to be nurses, worked by oil lamps. Some women moved to the city in order to work in munitions production.[198]

Mrs. Eugenia Bumpass continued:

Those things rationed by the government were gas, tires, recaps, sugar, coffee, and hose. Antibiotics were unavailable, sulphur was substituted. Prices were inflated. Citizens coped with these hardships at home and used stamps to support the war effort.[199]

The Role of Honor Board was erected on the courthouse lawn, listing the names of many of the Louisa residents who served in World War II. Names were submitted to the local newspaper to be entered on the board. *Courtesy of the Griswold Boxley Collection.*

After the war, the Town of Louisa looked to the future. An immediate need for the community was better medical care. The hospital was located in the old home of Dr. Henry Vaughan, a dentist, and was a private hospital run by Dr. Holmes G. Byrd.

On December 8, 1949, Henry Woolfolk's property was selected as the site of a new medical center. The land was a gift from members of T. Lafayette Woolfolk's family. The board of supervisors and the Memorial Medical Center accepted the Woolfolk location. A groundbreaking ceremony was attended by many citizens and officials on December 30, 1950.[200] H.M. Woodward, president of the board of trustees of the Medical Center; Dr. H.S. Daniel, representing the medical profession; and Carl H. Nolting, chairman of the board of supervisors, performed the breaking of the ground.[201] The Louisa County Memorial Medical Service Center opened in 1952.

In 1950, the town consisted of approximately 144 acres; the town proposed that 435 acres be annexed. This annexation expanded the town limits in all directions. After this annexation, in 1957, the Mineral Realty and Development Corporation bought land for a new development called Donnally Dale. The company bought a little over 50 acres of land that was owned originally by the Gooch family and was later owned by the Donnallys. New ranch-style houses were built and a community pool was constructed about 1976.

In January of 1972, the Virginia Power and Electric Company built a dam on the eastern edge of Louisa County to create the lake needed to build a nuclear power plant.

Main Street, Louisa, with the first Safeway building.

Hurricane Agnes swept through the region in June of 1972 and helped to fill up the 9,600-acre main body of what would become Lake Anna.[202] The hurricane expedited the building of the power plant, with additional help from Hurricane Camille three years earlier in another section. Construction on the nuclear units began in 1974 and 1975. North Anna Unit No. One went online in 1978. A strong tax break was introduced to the Louisa economy, encouraging an influx of residents who wanted to live on the lake. With new people came new businesses, and the small county began to grow. The town of Louisa also benefited greatly from the power plant.

On February 13, 1975, Judge Stewart A. Cunningham, a veteran of twenty-nine years on the bench, was presiding over the Louisa General District Court when he was shot to death by Curtis Darnell Poindexter. Poindexter wounded Sheriff Henry A. Kennon and Deputy Sheriff Charles Rosensohn. Both men survived.

Curtis Poindexter had been convicted by Judge Cunningham on a charge of speeding a month earlier. Curtis's father felt that his son had been pressured by a religious sect. Curtis Poindexter was sentenced to life in prison plus forty-seven years. He was tried in Rockbridge County.[203]

In 1977, another annexation took place that more than tripled the land area of the town. One development resulting from this annexation was the Tanyard Country Club and subdivision. The Tanyard Country Club is located on the property that was, in earlier times, the land of W.W. Beadles, whose family had resided just outside of the town since colonial times.

In 1955, Bruce Boxley's widow, Anna Griswold McIntosh Boxley, sold half interest in the *Central Virginian* to a longtime employee, Lewise Cosby, and they ran the newspaper

The Town of Louisa held a centennial celebration in May 1973. The wives of the town council and mayor served as hostesses in period costumes. *Left to right*: Mrs. Joseph N. Porter, Mrs. Mason Compton, Mrs. William C. Hart, Mrs. Ruth V. Boxley (official hostess, town clerk/treasurer), Centenial Queen Miss Linda Kaye Bailey, Mrs. Forrest Rosson (the town's first lady), Mrs. Robert A. Whitlock and Mrs. Robert E. Bailey. With the group are Porter C. Wright, Honorable V. Earl Dickinson and Mason Compton. *Courtesy of the* Central Virginian.

together until their deaths in 1987 and 1986 respectively.[204] The newspaper is still the *Central Virginian*, but in 1989 the CV Corporation was created by a consortium of local business leaders to purchase and operate the paper.[205] The corporation established the *Goochland Courier* and bought the *Herald Progress* based in Ashland. The three newspapers were acquired by Lakeway Publishers, Inc. in December of 2007.[206]

A movie company came to the town to film *Foreign Student* in the fall of 1992. A steam engine was brought to town for the film, which was set in the 1950s. The crew filmed first in the fall of 1992 and returned in the spring of 1993 to complete the filming. The members of the production company were composed mostly of Californians, who were dismayed by the greenery of spring, which created discontinuity in scenes from their fall shoot. They had to set up a line of cedar trees to obscure the abundant flowers. A scene from the movie *Toy Soldiers* was filmed at Louisa Courthouse, as well.

In 1990, the Virginia Board of Historic Resources placed the Louisa County Courthouse on the Virginia Landmarks Register. The courthouse remains the heart of the county, with several memorials to the past located on the lawn.

The 250th anniversary of Louisa County was celebrated in 1992 with a parade, a crafts fair, a published history, a ball and a finale that included fireworks and

The movie *Foreign Student* brought a steam engine to town. *Courtesy of the author.*

a concert provided by a military band on the courthouse lawn. Also, the 250th Anniversary Committee commissioned Steven M. Mickle to paint a portrait in pastels of Princess Louisa to grace a wall in the courthouse. Many portraits of people important to the history of Louisa County and to the town of Louisa can be found in the courthouse.

In 1998, the 125th Anniversary Committee celebrated the founding of the town of Louisa. The committee wanted to recognize the architectural growth particular to the town of Louisa by creating a walking tour. The tour focused on historical buildings, which are a tangible reminder of the growth of the town of Louisa around the county seat. The committee felt that a walking tour would expand, in town residents and in visitors, an appreciation of the past in general and of local culture specifically. Educating young people about the past better prepares them for the future. Louisa residents are better able to value the character of their town when they understand its history.

The town council, led by Mayor Charles Rosson, found a new location for the Louisa Town Hall. In the fall of 2002, the Town of Louisa purchased the Louisa High School (est. 1906) property and initiated plans to relocate the town hall to the historic Louisa High School building. The school has been restored and now contains business offices, community meeting rooms and a kitchen. In addition, the old school auditorium was expanded to facilitate a cinema and a community theater. Major donors to the project were recognized by having rooms named for them—the Purcell Gallery, the Cooke-Haley Theatre and the William A. Cooke Executive Conference Room.[207] The baseball diamond on the rear of the lot will continue to host local baseball games, and a seven-acre community park has been completed.

Since there is no major highway running through Louisa, the town is still reached by following twisting and turning roads. There are still gravel roads in the county. For many years, the town had only one stoplight, but in recent years three more stoplights and a bypass that allows motorists to avoid the Main Street area have been added. The passenger train stopped running years ago and the freight station closed in 1979. The closing of the freight station ended the anticipated delivery of oranges to Louisa at Christmastime. There is a small airport that is frequently used by sky divers in the county. Major shopping still means a trip to Richmond, Charlottesville or Fredericksburg. The town is still a step ahead of the rest of the county in receiving cable TV or computer DSL lines.

Louisa County still retains small communities that seem to be as close as family. Many people come to Louisa to retire. There are many craftspeople throughout the county and town. Louisa has long been known for its woodworkers, who produce fine furniture. In the town of Louisa, Mr. Aubrey Seay has specialized in quality woodworking for many years. His son Billie Seay has taken over since his father's retirement. Twin Oaks, a commune established in 1967, still remains one of the country's oldest communes. For many people, Louisa is still a place of opportunity for individual pursuits.

Chapter 17

The Future of the Town of Louisa

The current mayor of the town of Louisa, Jim Artz, was kind enough to give his impressions on the future of the town.

The future of the Town of Louisa is bright. As always, any predictions for the future are uncertain, but knowing the community, the area and the spirit of the town, I'm confident that despite some inevitable stumbles, the town will remain a strong center of government, population and growth within the county and Commonwealth of Virginia.

Today, the population of the Town of Louisa is just above 1,500 residents. We expect this number to grow substantially as two large subdivisions are built out. The 250 additional homes could increase our population to nearly 2,500 over the next few years, which will require expansion in public services offered such as water, sewer and solid waste management and of course an enhanced police presence. Additionally, expansion in the business sector providing restaurants, shopping, personal services, etc. will be needed to meet the needs of the current and future citizens.

In addition to the approved subdivisions, there is speculation that the North Anna Power Station may expand its operations, bringing several thousand transient workers in for the construction period and providing over seven hundred full-time jobs when construction is complete. While the plant is located outside of the town limits, surely some of that growth will be within the town limits due to the services the town provides and the convenience of living in the town environment.

The future is a challenge and one that must be carefully planned to ensure that the town's character and historic fabric is not lost. Luckily, we have dedicated elected public officials, professional staff and a myriad of citizen volunteers to serve on boards and commissions that look out for the best interest of the community.

Notes

Chapter 1

1. William Waller Hening, *The Statutes At Large, being a collection of all the laws of Virginia, from the first session of the legislature, in the year 1619*, vol. 5 (Richmond, VA: R&W&G Bartow, 1819–23), 208.
2. Milton Rubican, F.A.S.G, *Princess Louisa, Louisa County's Royal Namesake* (West Hyattsville, MD: 1970), 4.
3. Edna Harris Bushnell and Dr. James J. Bushnell, "Sheriff Joseph Bickley and the First Jail," *Louisa County Historical Society Magazine* 22 (1991): 91.
4. County of Louisa, *Louisa County Deed Books*, Louisa County Courthouse, Louisa, Virginia, A/237. Hereafter cited as LCDB.
5. Ibid., A/234.
6. LCDB, part 2, A/532.

Chapter 2

7. County of Louisa, *Louisa County Chancery Suits*, Louisa County Courthouse, Louisa, Virginia, case *Arnette v. Cammack*, 1891-023 and 1895-014.
8. Ransome True, *Land Transactions in Louisa County, 1765–1812* (Charlottesville, VA: University of Virginia Press, 1976), 33.
9. Malcolm H. Harris, *A History of Louisa County* (Richmond, VA: The Dietz Press Incorporated, 1936), 125.
10. V.M.S. English, *The Parson's Cause Case: Patrick Henry Becomes An Orator* (Ashland, VA: published by the author), 7.
11. Henning, *Statutes at Large*, vol. 5, 211.
12. Harris, *Louisa County*, 33.
13. Ibid., 21.
14. George Morgan, *The True Patrick Henry* (London: J.B. Lippincott, 1907), 114.
15. Ibid., 115.
16. Janice L. Abercrombie, "Abstracts of Judgment Papers," *Louisa County Historical Society Magazine* 20, no. 2 (1989): 92.

Chapter 3

17. Harris, *Louisa County*, 439.
18. Ibid., 51.
19. Ibid., 62.
20. True, *Land Transactions*, 81.
21. Ibid., 40.
22. Ibid., 54.
23. County of Louisa, *County of Louisa Order Books*, Louisa, Virginia, Louisa County Courthouse, 1781, 40. Hereafter cited as LCOB.

Chapter 4

24. Marquis De Chastellux, *Travels in North America, in the years 1780, 1781 and 1782*, Vol. 2, trans. Howard C. Rice Jr. (Chapel Hill: University of North Carolina Press, 1963), 572.
25. Ibid., 386–387.
26. LCDB, Book 4, 40.
27. *Louisa County Historical Society Magazine* 5 (1972): 22.
28. Harris, *Louisa County*, 137.
29 True, *Land Transactions*, 36.
30. LCOB, 1788–1790, 2.
31. Ibid., 5.

Chapter 5

32. James B. Taylor, *Virginia Baptist Ministers* (Philadelphia: J.B. Lippincott, 1895), 294–98.
33. LCDB J, 390.
34. LCDB K, 226.
35. True, *Land Transactions*, 37.
36. Ibid., 39.
37. Ibid.

Chapter 6

38. LCDB L, 53.
39. LCDB L, 44–45.
40. LCDB M, 631–632.
41. "Mutual Assurance Policy 465," reel 4, Virginia State Library, microfilm.
42. LCOB, June 10, 1816.
43. LCDB N, 173–174.
44. Ibid.
45. Town of Louisa, *Town of Louisa City Council Minutes*, Louisa Town Hall, Louisa, Virginia, 1826, 307. Hereafter cited as LTCM.
46. LCOB, 329.
47. LCDB O, 80.

48. LCDB O, 174.
49. U.S. National Archives. *Record of Appointments for Postmasters*, 1832, Microfilm Publication M841, September 30, 1971.
50. James W. Wright, "Private Schools in Louisa County," *Louisa County Historical Society Magazine* 25, no. 1 (1994): 26.
51. LTCM, 1845, 407.
52. LCDB P, 255.
53. LCDB R, 520.
54. LCDB Q, 15, March 1824.
55. LCDB T, 76, March 20, 1830.
56. LTCM, 522–23.
57. LCOB, 1809–1828, October 18, 1826, 301–02.
58. LTCM, 1831–1835, April 10, 1832, 128.
59. LCDB U, 49.

Chapter 7

60. *Arnette v. Cammack*, 1891-23.
61. Ibid.
62. Ibid.
63. Ibid.
64. George Bartton Cutten, *Silversmiths of Virginia* (Richmond, VA: The Dietz Press Incorporated, 1952), 59.
65. *Louisa Weekly Record*, May 13, 1876.
66. Harris, *Louisa County*, 146.
67. Ibid., 147.
68. *Central Virginian*, July 1938.
69. Ibid. 34.
70. Wright, "Private Schools in Louisa County," 26.

Chapter 8

71. Janice L. Abercrombie, comp., *Louisa County, Virginia Death Records, 1853–1896* (Athens, GA: Iberian Publishing Company, 1997), 17.
72. Ibid., 273–74.
73. Edmund and Kathleen Meredith, *St. James Episcopal Church, 1881–1991* (Louisa, VA: 1981), 16.
74. LCDB X, 496–98.
75. *Arnette v. Cammack*, deposition by Hugh Cullen.
76. Ibid.
77. Courthouse store ledger from June 1844, Louisa County Courthouse, Louisa, Virginia.
78. LCOB, 368.
79. Louisa County Chancery case *Levy v. Levy*, 1858-002.
80. LCDB AA, Stout to Gooch, July 24, 1846, 4.

81. LCDB AA, December 11, 1846, 92.
82. Harvey L. Fleshman, "Masonry in Virginia and Louisa County," *Louisa County Historical Society Magazine* 20, no. 2 (1989): 77.
83. Ibid.; Harvey L. Fleshman, "Worshipful Masters of Day Lodge no. 58, Louisa, Va." *Louisa County Historical Society Magazine* 20, no. 2 (1989): 79.
84. Wright, "Private Schools in Louisa County," 26.
85. "Wm F Cox [24]" appears in the 1860 list as a tailor.
86. Harris, *Louisa County*, 229.
87. LCDB CC, 620–27.
88. Ibid.

Chapter 9

89. LCDB EE, 453.
90. James Roger Mansfield, *A History of Early Spotsylvania* (Orange, VA: Green Publishers, Inc., 1977), 200.
91. LCDB EE, 599.
92. LCDB FF, January 17, 1861, 214.
93. Ibid.
94. Wright, "Private Schools in Louisa County," 29.

Chapter 10

95. Walbrook Davis Swank, *The War and Louisa County, 1861–1865* (Charlottesville, VA: Papercraft Printing and Design Company, 1986), preface.
96. Harris, *Louisa County*, 212.
97. David F. Riggs, *13th Virginia Infantry* (Lynchburg, VA: H.E. Howard, Inc., 1988), 1.
98. Ibid.; courthouse ledger written in 1902.
99. LCOB, 1860, 734.
100. Virginia Central Rail Road (VCRR) Superintendent's Report, microfilm, 1856.
101. Ibid., 1862.
102. Ibid.
103. Carter S. Anderson, "Train Running for the Confederacy," *Locomotive Engineering* (July 1892 and January 1898): 7–9.
104. Walbrook Davis Swank's description of the raid, from *Louisa County History* (Shippensburg, PA: Burd Street Press, 1994), 47.

Chapter 11

105. Walbrook Davis Swank's description of the Battle of Trevilian Station, with eyewitness memoirs, in *Louisa County History*, 86–87.
106. Ibid., memoir of Lieutenant Alfred Aldrich, 86.
107. Swank, *War and Louisa County*, 98.
108. Ibid.
109. Ibid.
110. Ibid.

111. Ibid., 96.
112. *Louisa Advance*, February 14, 1890.
113. "Lindsay Gordon Lauds Dr. Joe Baker," *Central Virginian*, September 18, 1980.
114. VCRR Superintendent's Report, 1865.
115. Ibid.

Chapter 12

116. LCOB, March 30, 1869, 476.
117. Nancy C. Baird, "Letters of Major General Alvin Coe Voris," *Louisa County Historical Society Magazine* 19, no. 2 (1988): 81–85.
118. Ibid., 82.
119. Ibid., 83.
120. Ibid., 84.
121. Ibid., 85.
122. Nancy C. Baird, "Letters of Major General Alvin Coe Voris," *Louisa County Historical Society Magazine* 20, no. 1, 1988, 53.
123. Ibid., 54.
124. *The 130th Anniversary of the First Baptist Church* (Louisa, VA: 1996).
125. John Mercer Langston, *From the Virginia Plantation to the National Capitol, An Autobiography* (New York: Bergman Publishers, 1969), 267–74.
126. Ibid.
127. *Times Dispatch*, Richmond, Virginia, Sunday, August 13, 1905.
128. Albert Ogden Porter, *County Government in Virginia* (New York: AMS Press, Inc., 1966), 243.

Chapter 13

129. Pearl Mills Harris, *A Brief History of Education in Louisa County* (Orange, VA: The Orange Review, 1963), 19.
130. Claudia Chisholm, "The Reverend Littleberry Haley Diary," *Louisa County Historical Society Magazine* 4, no. 1 (1972): 18.
131. Harris, *A Brief History*, 19.
132. Chisholm, "The Reverend Littleberry Haley Diary," 81.
133. Paul Behrens, *A Survey of Negro Education in Louisa County* (Charlottesville: University of Virginia Press, 1949), 13.
134. Virginia General Assembly Act, March 8, 1873.
135. LTCM.
136. 250th Anniversary Committee, *Louisa County, Virginia, 250th Anniversary* (Louisa, VA: 250th Anniversary Committee, 1992),124.
137. Ibid.
138. Ibid.
139. *The 130th Anniversary of the First Baptist Church.*
140. Harris, *A Brief History*, 55–56.

Chapter 14

141. *Free Lance Star*, Fredericksburg, January 1888.
142. *Arnette v. Cammack*, 1891-23.
143. LTCM, April 1893.
144. Peter Wallenstein, "The Case of the Laborer from Louisa: Three Central Virginians and the Origins of the Virginia Highway System." *The Magazine of Albemarle County History* 49 (1991): 19–47.
145. 250th Anniversary Committee, *Louisa County, Virginia*, 124.

Chapter 15

146. Louis L. Kean, "Louisa Telephone Company, Chartered 1898," *Louisa County Historical Society Magazine* 19, no. 1 (1988): 45.
147. Ibid.
148. LTCM, October 8, 1903.
149. LCDB 22, 256, July 6, 1904.
150. *Times Dispatch*, Richmond, Virginia, August 13, 1905.
151. Ibid., July 7, 1909.
152. Louisa County Chancery case, 1928-156.
153. LTCM, September 15, 1909.
154. County of Louisa, *County of Louisa Supervisor's Journal*, Louisa County Courthouse, Louisa, Virginia, no. 2, 310.
155. *Louisa County News.*
156. *Louisa Enterprise*, August 1905.
157. Porter Clay Wright, "History of the Town of Louisa," *Louisa County Historical Society Magazine* 29, no. 1 (1973): 9–10.
158. *Central Virginian*, August 20, 1931.
159. Supervisor's Journal, no. 1, 12.
160. LTCM, vol. 2.
161. Ibid., September 7, 1906, 27–28.
162. *Central Virginian*, April 15, 1926.
163. Ibid., 12.
164. Harris, *A Brief History*, 39.
165. LTCM, 1906, 40.
166. Louisa County Chancery case, 1928-156.
167. Harris, *A Brief History*, 56.
168. Pattie Cooke, *Louisa County History, A Cooperative Effort* (Louisa, VA: Louisa Printing, 1997), 90.
169. LTCM, 72.
170. Supervisor's Journal, no. 5, 235.
171. 250th Anniversary Committee, *Louisa County, Virginia*, 124.
172. LTCM, 1914, 84.
173. Helen Waltman, "The *Central Virginian* salutes Mr. and Mrs. Manning Woodward," *Central Virginian*, February 25, 1982.

174. Ibid., May 31, 1915, 88.
175. *Central Virginian*, 1945.
176. Ibid., June 21, 1915, 88.
177. LTCM, December 2, 1919.
178. LTCM, April 1, 1918, 115.
179. Louisa County Clerk's Office, War Records, Louisa County Courthouse, Louisa, Virginia.
180. Ann Cottrell, "George McDuffie Blake," *Louisa County Historical Society Magazine* 27, no. 1 (1996): 8.
181. LTCM, April 24, 1923.
182. Pat Wilson, *Central Virginian*, June 23, 2005.
183. Ibid., June 11, 1936.
184. Ibid.
185. Richard E. Conover, *Give'em a John Robinson: A documentary on the old John Robinson Circus* (Xenia, OH: Published by author, 1965).
186. Ibid.
187. Ibid.
188. Ibid.
189. *Central Virginian*, November 20, 1930.
190. Swank, *Louisa County History*, 77.
191. Hattie Crebbs, interview, April 2008.
192. LTCM, September 2, 1919.
193. 250th Anniversary Committee, *Louisa County, Virginia*, 122.
194. *Central Virginian*, March 16, 1995.
195. Louisa County Chancery case, 1937-071.

Chapter 16

196. Cooke, *Louisa County History, A Cooperative Effort*, Mrs. Netty Trainum, 90.
197. Ibid.
198. Ibid., Mrs. Anna Seay.
199. Ibid., Mrs. Eugenia Bumpass.
200. The *Central Virginian*, December 30, 1950.
201. Ibid.
202. *Central Virginian*, August 28, 1997.
203. John O. Peters and Margaret T. Peters, *Virginia's Historic Courthouses* (Charlottesville: University of Virginia Press, 1995), 196.
204. *Central Virginian*, December 27, 2007, A-10.
205. Ibid.
206. Ibid.
207. *Central Virginian*, March 6, 2008.

Bibliography

The 130th Anniversary of the First Baptist Church. Louisa, VA: 1996.

250th Anniversary Committee. *Louisa County, Virginia, 250th Anniversary*. Louisa, VA: 250th Anniversary Committee, 1992

Abercrombie, Janice L. "Abstracts of Judgement Papers." *Louisa County Historical Society Magazine* 20, no. 2 (1989).

———., comp. *Louisa County, Virginia Death Records, 1853–1896.* Athens, GA: Iberian Publishing Company, 1997.

Anderson, Carter S. "Train Running for the Confederacy." *Locomotive Engineering* (July 1892 and January 1898).

Baird, Nancy C. "Letters of Major Generel Alvin Coe Voris." *Louisa County Historical Society Magazine* 19, no. 2 (1988).

———. "Letters of Major Generel Alvin Coe Voris." *Louisa County Historical Society Magazine* 20, no. 1 (1988).

Behrens, Paul. *A Survey of Negro Education in Louisa County.* Charlottesville: University of Virginia Press, 1949.

Bushnell, Edna Harris, and Dr. James J. Bushnell. "Sheriff Joseph Bickley and the First Jail." *Louisa County Historical Society Magazine* 22, no. 2 (1991).

Chisholm, Claudia. "The Reverend Littleberry Haley Diary." *Louisa County Historical Society Magazine* 4, no. 1 (1972).

Conover, Richard E. *Giv'em a John Robinson: A documentary on the old John Robinson Circus*. Xenia, OH: published by author, 1965.

Cooke, Pattie. *Louisa County History, A Cooperative Effort.* Louisa, VA: Louisa Publishing, 1997.

Cottrell, Ann. "George McDuffie Blake." *Louisa County Historical Society Magazine* 27, no. 1 (1996).

County of Louisa. *County of Louisa Chancery Suits*. Louisa County Courthouse. Louisa, Virginia.

———. *County of Louisa Deed Books.* Louisa County Courthouse. Louisa, Virginia.

———. *County of Louisa Order Books*. Louisa County Courthouse. Louisa, Virginia.

———. *County of Louisa Supervisor's Journal*. Louisa County Courthouse. Louisa, Virginia.

Cutten, George Bartton. *Silversmiths of Virginia.* Richmond, VA: The Dietz Press Incorporated, 1952.

De Chastellux, Marquis. *Travels in North America, in the years 1780, 1781 and 1782*. Vol. 2. Translated by Howard C. Rice Jr. Chapel Hill: University of North Carolina Press, 1963.

English, V.M.S. *The Parson's Cause Case: Patrick Henry Becomes An Orator.* Ashland, VA: published by the author.

Fleshman, Harvey L. "Masonry in Virginia and Louisa County." *Louisa County Historical Society Magazine* 20, no. 2 (1989).

———. "Worshipful Masters of Day Lodge no. 58, Louisa, Va." *Louisa County Historical Society Magazine* 20, no. 2 (1989).

Harris, Malcolm H. *A History of Louisa County*, Richmond, VA: The Dietz Press Incorporated, 1936.

Harris, Pearl Mills. *A Brief History of Education in Louisa County*. Orange, VA: The Orange Review, 1963.

Hening, William Waller. *The Statutes At Large, being a collection of all the laws of Virginia, from the first session of the legislature, in the year 1619*. Vol. 5. Richmond, VA: R&W&G Bartow, 1819–23.

Kean, Louis L. "Louisa Telephone Company, Chartered 1898." *Louisa County Historical Society Magazine* 19, no. 1 (1988).

Langston, John Mercer. *From the Virginia Plantation to the National Capitol, An Autobiography.* New York: Bergman Publishers, 1969.

Mansfield, James Roger. *A History of Early Spotsylvania.* Orange, VA: Green Publishers, Inc., 1977.

Meredith, Edmund, and Kathleen Meredith. *St. James Episcopal Church, 1881–1991.* Louisa, VA: 1981.

Morgan, George. *The True Patrick Henry.* London: J.B. Lippincott, 1907.

Peters, John O., and Margaret T. Peters. *Virginia's Historic Courthouses.* Charlottesville: University of Virginia Press, 1995.

Porter, Albert Ogden. *County Government in Virginia.* New York: AMS Press, Inc., 1966.

Riggs, David F. *13th Virginia Infantry.* Lynchburg, VA: H.E. Howard, Inc., 1988.

Rubicam, Milton, F.A.S.G. *Princess Louisa, Louisa County's Royal Namesake.* West Hyattsville, MD: 1970.

Swank, Walbrook Davis. *Louisa County History.* Shippensburg, PA: Burd Street Press, 1994.

———. *The War and Louisa County, 1861–1865.* Charlottesville, VA: Papercraft Printing and Design Company, 1986.

Taylor, James B. *Virginia Baptist Ministers.* Philadelphia: J.B. Lippincott, 1859.

Town of Louisa. *Town of Louisa City Council Minutes.* Louisa Town Hall. Louisa, Virginia.

True, Ransome. *Land Transactions in Louisa County, 1765–1812.* Charlottesville: University of Virginia Press, 1976.

U.S. National Archives. *Record of Appointment for Postmasters, 1832.* Microfilm Publication M841. September 30, 1971.

Virginia Central Rail Road Superintendent's Report. Microfilm. 1856.

———. Microfilm. 1862.

Wallenstein, Peter. "The Case of the Laborer from Louisa: Three Central Virginians and the Origins of the Virginia Highway System." *The Magazine of Albemarle County History* 49 (1991).

Wright, James W. "Private Schools in Louisa County." *Louisa County Historical Society Magazine* 25, no. 1 (1994).

Wright, Porter Clay. "History of the Town of Louisa." *Louisa County Historical Society Magazine* 29, no. 1 (1998).